THE
MASTER

Beside yon straggling fence that skirts the way,
With blossom'd furze unprofitably gay,
There, in his noisy mansion, skilled to rule,
The village master taught his little school.
A man severe he was, and stern to view;
I knew him well, and every truant knew:
Well had the boding tremblers learn'd to trace
The day's disasters in his morning face;
Full well they laugh'd with counterfeited glee
At all his jokes, for many a joke had he;
Full well the busy whisper, circling round,
Convey'd the dismal tidings when he frown'd.
Yet he was kind; or if severe in aught,
The love he bore to learning was in fault.

—Goldsmith (*The Deserted Village*)

THE
MASTER
BRYAN MACMAHON

POOLBEG

First published 1992 by
Poolbeg
A Division of Poolbeg Enterprises Ltd
Knocksedan House,
Swords, Co Dublin, Ireland
This edition 1993

Reprinted September 1993

Poolbeg Press receives assistance from
the Arts Council /An Chomhairle Ealaíon, Ireland.

ISBN 1 85371 254 X

A catalogue record for this book is available from the British Library

Cover design by Poolbeg
Cover photograph courtesy of Kevin Coleman, *The Kerryman*
Set by Mac Book Limited in Stone Serif 9.5/15
Printed by The Guernsey Press Company Limited,
Vale, Guernsey, Channel Islands.

For Maurice and Yvonne

A Note on the Author

Bryan MacMahon is one of Ireland's most distinguished writers. He has written novels, plays, ballads and collections of short stories. His historical pageant *A Pageant of Ireland* ran for sixteen years in a medieval castle in Clare and was seen by over half a million people. He lives in Listowel, County Kerry.

CHAPTER ONE

Where in the name of Heaven had the ferret got to?

Cupping my hands about my eyes, I looked through the window of the presbytery parlour. There, balanced on the back of the armchair, was the bald head of the old canon; in the backround of the room was seated a woman whose features I could not discern clearly. Of the ferret there was no trace.

The rabbit-trapper and I had been asked by the curate to catch some rats in the garden of the old presbytery. Here we were with the ferret missing underground. I searched the shrubbery where the rat-holes were. Again I went to the window and looked in. To my horror I saw the ferret emerge from a hole in the wainscot and walk coolly along the little ledge, his gentle nose sniffing the air, his long, silken cream-and-brown body following him obediently.

"I'll be back in a moment," I said as I raced away.

I had been an altar boy who served Mass into his teens, so I knew my way around the presbytery. In by the back door I raced and through the kitchen, then up some steps leading to the canon's parlour. I barely knocked on the door, then with a quick "Excuse me" stretched behind the canon's head and took the ferret in my hand.

The woman in the room spoke up. I knew the voice well: it was that of my mother, then a teacher in the local school.

"Here he is, canon," she said. "I hope you won't refuse him the appointment."

The ferret dangling from my hand, I turned. Appointment? I wanted no appointment. I already had a teaching job in Dublin and was happy enough with it.

The old canon turned his head. "I'll give you the position," he wheezed.

I was flabbergasted. I went out with the ferret hanging from my hand.

When my mother returned home there was a battle royal. I was going to stay on in Dublin, I told her. I was going to study at the university. I was not going to be "cabined, cribbed, confined" in the small town of Listowel. I had had a bellyful of small places.

Patiently, my mother wore me down. I could be as happy— perhaps happier—in a country town, she told me. After a sharp struggle her wisdom prevailed; thus began the long sojourn in the town of my birth, which, with certain interludes, has lasted to the present day.

I had been off school for some weeks on sick leave—suspected pleurisy contracted after being drenched to the skin while queuing on a bitter winter night to see a Jimmy O'Dea revue in the Olympia Theatre in Dublin. Much against my will, I wrote my letter of resignation to the school in Dublin and prepared to present myself to the local school. The year was 1931.

My term spent teaching in the Dublin Liberties had suggested that I had some talent in the classroom. I was resolved to exploit it in my own idiom. My mother as a young woman had taught in Lancashire for ten years; she had come home to marry my father, then a clerk in a law office, and later to take up a local teaching appointment. To us four children she transferred an international outlook on events, flashes of unusual teaching techniques, a smattering of Scouse, and an insight into the mysterious world of Ouija boards and planchettes as a means of probing the future. Long after leaving Lancashire she continued to send for fashionable clothes to Lewis's of Market Street, Manchester. I often wonder how my Gaelic League father viewed this unpatriotic practice!

I was little more than an infant when my mother drove me in an ass and trap to Clounmacon, a country school some three miles north-west of Listowel, where she first taught on her return to Ireland. I was perhaps three years of age at the time and was dressed in a blue velvet suit with a lace collar—also from Lewis's of Manchester. I was then given into the control and care of a bunch of nubile girls in the senior classes. They hugged me and kissed me and pressed me to their bosoms, giving me my first vague consciousness of the secret possibilities of womanhood.

Nowadays, whatever way I turn in my self-assessment, I seem always to have been in school. The memory of that first school abides with me still. First the catching of the donkey as I grew older; he kicked me once in the stomach—a little black ass, much like the one Pádraic Ó Conaire had. The journey to school was an adventure. There was the woodbine growing above a cottage hedge, apples peeping over the orchard wall of the demesne; later in the year holly berries proclaimed Christmas. I saw a mud house being made, heard boycott horns being sounded, and saw Volunteers being drilled with hurleys on their shoulders.

Teaching was in my blood. Three of my mother's sisters had been teachers; so was my brother Jack; two of my own sons are now teachers in different levels of education.

The love of learning had been passed on in the locality by the old hedge-school masters Dinny Dillane and the Bachall Stack, and the classical tradition was still carried on in St Michael's College, where I was fortunate to come under the influence of Séamus Wilmot, a teacher of infectious enthusiasm who fired in me the passion of writing. I had the benefit of Tim O'Connor's broad mind, while Irish was taught in all its purity by Mícheál O'Sullivan, a native speaker from near Glengarriff.

With the Civil War following on the War of Independence, and the senior boys taking sides, there was always a revolver or two in the classroom, but the teachers took all this in their stride; it was part of the background of shooting and bombing prevailing at that hour.

At home I created a fuss to be allowed sit an examination for the Indian civil service, because a local man, Sir Michael Keane, had become governor of Assam. My motives were certainly not colonial: I foresaw that the day of freedom for India could not be long delayed; I would then opt to remain on to assist in the rebirth of a great nation. There were Irish parallels for this. I wrote to Trinity College, Dublin, for the relevant papers, and kept them hidden.

But my mother had other ideas, and insisted on my sitting the King's Scholarship examination for admission to training as a national teacher; eventually I qualified from St Patrick's College, Drumcondra, Dublin. Studying and the onerous duties as senior prefect made my stay a doleful one that at times threatened to undermine my health.

The first part of my short teaching term in Dublin I spent in digs in Rathmines. The area was still quaint and genteel. The young women in the civil service gave parties—much like the one described in Joyce's story "The Dead." The boys I taught in Donore Avenue, off the South Circular Road, were excellent children; it was a newly built-up area, and it seemed that everyone was determined to reach a high standard of respectability.

I began to shadow William Butler Yeats each evening as he walked through the streets on his way to the Abbey Theatre, in an effort to discover what "made him tick." I realised, even then, that around him hung an aura of eminence.

There is no adequate word to describe the squalor of the Dublin slums that persisted into the thirties. You had to hold your nose as you passed through the meaner streets. So I saw poverty-stricken Ireland in the city as well as in the small town. By way of contrast, when I returned to Listowel the fairs and markets were in the height of their glory.

My grandfather was "weighmaster and marketkeeper," in charge of the market yard and its environment. To me the place onto which our back gate opened was like an eastern bazaar. It seemed always thronged with farmers, buyers, labourers, roustabouts, pedlars, politicians, quack doctors, old-clothes sellers, showmen, and conmen. All kinds of farm animals and farm produce were offered for sale. There were also seasonable visits from circuses and bazaars, and even dancing bears. And I can recall the recruiting sergeant in scarlet uniform and tall black bearskin hat moving through the throng.

As a boy I had often been left in charge of this wonderful area—that was when my grandfather left the office to have a drink with a farmer friend. At an early age I was taught how to weigh cartloads of mangels and turnips, and how to deduct the tare; I would then issue a ticket to verify that the weight was correct.

My background was not very different from that of many of my charges, for directly or indirectly the livelihood of their parents was bound up with the market and the fair. I also learnt to use the splendid rhetoric of that vivid place. All the while catchcries were ringing in my head; but for me as a teacher the Davis quotation "We must educate that we may be free" seemed most worthy of being borne in mind. An ideal that I tried to transfer to my pupils, even in devious or simplified form, was that in the Ireland of the future there would be only one aristocracy: not that of privilege or birth but that of ability.

In the temporary accommodation of the old St Patrick's Temperance Hall, with two older teachers and 140 boys competing for air, sound, and floor space, I began to teach my huddle of scholars beside the grimy window that looked out directly onto the street. Every head passing on the pavement outside turned to gawk in at me.

I looked at my class. Many were barefoot, their toes bloodied, scabbed, and bruised. Some affluent children—sons of bank officials, well-off merchants and farmers—seemed to be exceptions.

Some of the lads were comparatively old. One boy in particular was fifteen or sixteen; he had remained on in school to be confirmed. It was a morning of driving rain, and placing my hand on this lad's jacket, which I found to be sodden, I said, "Take off your coat, son, and hang it before the fire"—there was a fire of sorts, smoky sods, wholly inadequate for heating the great hall. The boy looked up at me squarely. "I won't," he said. He was almost as big as myself. "Why not?" "I won't take off my coat for you, nor for anyone." I then realised that, like Larry of the old tale, the boy had not much of a shirt to his back. I did not argue the matter further. Without asking permission to leave, he then tramped out the front door and, squatting on a kerbstone at the end of the building and in full view of the passers-by, he reddened his clay pipe and began to puff contentedly.

That afternoon I took stock of my situation. What had I got myself into? A life sentence in a backwater?

It was a time of dreadful squalor. The Free State had been established only nine years before, and this had been followed by a bitter civil war. Before that the struggle for freedom had overlapped the slaughter of the First World War. Before that again stretched centuries of colonial exploitation. The hills I could view through the dingy school window were replete with the balladry of an outlawed people, and echoed to the sound of traditional music and the ring of a delightful dialect.

I had been told I could write. I had read a great deal at this time; I was subscribing to poetry magazines in America and Britain and procuring books from many sources. I had long since decided that within the confines of the community in which I found myself I would push myself to the limit of mind and body. A quotation from a Russian master continually occurred to me: "If you're born with a tarred rope in your hand, pull it."

I look at the dim class photographs of that time with misgivings. Disease was implied in the pale faces before me. Infant mortality was taken for granted. The white coffin slung on ribbons and carried through the streets by huge ex-soldiers was almost an everyday sight. Pneumonia was feared; the crisis time struck terror. But despite adversity, the boys before me seemed poised to leap forward, eager to bring about change.

After a month or two we left the temporary accommodation in

the temperance hall and returned to the "renovated" school. To use a modern term, it was a failed cosmetic exercise. A barbarous building, it had been described by the scholar Alfred O'Rahilly— a one-time pupil of the same school who later became president of University College, Cork, and later still became a priest—as "a barracks built upon a cesspool." And so it remained from his boyhood up to the time when, with my gaggle of students, I faced into it again in 1931.

The building had been opened in 1836 and so was ten years in existence when the famine carts began to go out from the local workhouse every morning to collect the dead for burial in Teampaillín Bán, a plot that in recent years has become cherished by the local people.

Yet humanity is blessed, or cursed, with the ability to accept the abnormal as normal. Probably this is one of the chief methods of animal survival. Even in my time everyone seemed to think it was what ought to be, and baulked even at having it discussed. Odd as it now sounds, it seemed normal that children should have dirty, bloody bare feet, that lice should crawl over their jackets, that flea-marks should pock their bodies, that they should be hungry and poor. Infantile death was something to be accepted as God's will and even occasionally welcomed for the eternal merit it promised.

But adversity also contains at its core the pricking of action. For this was also a time of idealism: much of the fervour of the Easter Rising persisted into the twenties and thirties; the wave of consumerism and materialism, with its attendant revision of our island story, had not yet threatened to engulf us.

We realised that without a vision the people perished. We realised that there was nowhere the children could move on the social ladder except upwards. Personally, I realised that motivation was a first requisite if the lost children of the nation were to be cherished. So we set out to establish something bright and shining, in which the Irish language would play an important part.

Speaking about an old schoolmaster, someone once said to me that a good teacher leaves the print of his teeth on a parish for three generations. I realised that each child had a gift, and that the "leading out" of that gift was the proper goal of teaching. To me a great teacher was simply a great person teaching.

I aim to speak for thousands of other teachers, most of them largely unsung: for my mother, who endured the same dire conditions as I did; for my brother, who taught in a large school for deprived children in Rutland Street, Dublin; and for thousands of unknown teachers in small, substandard schools up and down the country.

First of all, I was resolved to praise, for "Mol an óige agus tiocfaidh sí; cáin an óige agus críonfaidh sí"—praise youth and it will come; disparage youth and it will wither. An instrument of education, that's what I would be. I would read everything I could lay my hands on. I would establish contact with the literature of other lands, while holding faith with what was worthy in my own country.

Latin and Greek gave us dimensions on the human being that we would not otherwise have received. Latin had always intrigued me. I had spent an hour a day for seven years learning Greek; too late I realised that the cream of that discipline had already been expended on Latin.

Education, as I knew then, though primitive was good up to a point, but it should also have provided a stepping-stone to action. At times it can be a confidence trick played by unseen puppetmasters on parents and children.

I had attended the same school—two separate schools under one roof—as a pupil; but when one is a barefoot lad and the summer is replete with the excitement of grenades bursting in the streets and bullets whining past, added to which was our hysterical laughter as we youngsters raced home before curfew, the school building does not seem to matter. It seemed part of the warp and woof of our boyhood.

Now, as a teacher, I viewed it with hostile eyes. A large pool of stagnant water reposed at the side of the gate as one entered. When an inspector commented adversely on the pool I turned back the pages of an old report book and showed that the same pool had been adversely commented on in the 1870s.

Water from this pool seeped under the building, rendering it perpetually damp. Beyond this pool was a toilet of sorts with a great water tank overhead. The three open cubicles were in a perpetual state of dampness and enormously soiled. There was one toilet equipped with a door for all the teachers, male and female. The building itself was grim; four windows upstairs and four downstairs were set in naked limestone facing north.

There was one tap for some 350 children. The handle of the tap had long since snapped off, so that the water seemed either perpetually running or perpetually cut off. Strong pliers could sometimes get movement—off or on—from the tap. Nine times out of ten the water overflowed the metal trough and poured down into the hallway. Thence it seeped into the locked-up area beneath the stairwell, where a single rail of turf was stored for the miserable school fires.

Heating and cleaning in the school were almost non-existent. The cleaning was done by poorer boys kept in after school (well-off parents would complain if their children were set this task), who sprinkled water on the floors and brushed amid a cloud of dust. The lavatories were Augean stables in miniature. The boys never sat on the open toilets: they squatted on top of the seats and deliberately soiled the boards so as to avoid the vile splash, with the result that each afternoon there was an accumulation of faeces for the poorer boys to shovel into the lavatory bowls and flush away. A later improvement on this operation was the use of a garden hose assisted by brushes. As gangers-in-charge, the principal of the adjoining school and I were dab hands with the hose.

The fireplaces were holes in the wall into which damp turf was dumped. It took an hour or more before the fire reddened, but little or no heat came forth: there really was smoke without fire. In the interests of safety, fireguards were introduced at some stage. On a wet day the fireguards were festooned with steaming sodden clothes. The desks were long and had holes containing pottery inkwells. The ink we made ourselves out of ink powder; for obvious reasons the inkwells were a source of constant amusement to the children.

The twenty pounds allocated to each school per year for heating and cleaning was grossly inadequate. We had no caretaker, little running water, less light, no heat—just one squalid mess.

There now began a parochial war to have this building replaced. One prominent parent threatened publicly to set fire to the building. As if the wet turf in the fireplace had overheard the threat, it dropped a smouldering sod on the floor at midnight and burned a circle out of the boards. And then, to my sorrow, it went out.

My mother taught in the room beneath me. The number of infants in her class was an incredible 120 when all her pupils were present. When she murmured to the curate about the number of pupils she had to teach she was told that she was lucky to have so many: did she realise that certain schools in the country were closing because of falling averages?

Needless to say, this burden took its toll on my mother's health. I accompanied her when she visited a heart specialist in Dublin; she was told bluntly that she would die if she continued teaching. Her reply was that she had to retain her post to see her own children educated. At this time my father was an invalid. She returned home knowing that she was doomed, yet continued teaching. The infants in my mother's class, crawling and sprawling on the floor, with the lavatory and its stench a bare eight feet from her window, had pulled the loose threads from the hem of her skirt. Day after day this went on until finally she was wearing a garment not unlike the mini-skirt. In time she suffered a stroke, and lingered for years in a twilight world, with my sister Máirín as devoted nurse.

The young English-trained teacher who replaced my mother and who was to spend her own teaching life in the school could scarcely believe the numbers she had inherited. I wished her a better fate than that my mother had met with.

This was the kind of place where the teachers of the thirties were ordered to embark on a great scholastic adventure under one of the first native governments. What would keep me going? I asked myself. And whence was I to draw motivation? I drew it from something that happened surely fourteen years before this, when I was a pupil in the same old school.

One afternoon there came a knock on the classroom door. Opened, it revealed a smiling man wearing spectacles, with a freckled face and sandy hair. I had already seen him talking to my father in Irish, but I could not recall his name. Our teacher invited him in. Some words passed between the two men; to our surprise the teacher suddenly left the room, leaving the stranger standing before us. He spoke in the language I had already heard from my grandmother, who had precious little English. "Dia is Muire daoibh," he said. No answer. He repeated the greeting. I piped up with, "Dia is Muire duit is Pádraig." "No-one else can answer?" Then, "Children, what language would you hear if you visited France?" "French," we chorused. In response to similar queries, "Spanish," "Italian" and "Greek" came our replies in turn. Then, "In Ireland?—Irish?" "No—English." "But you have a language of your own," the visitor said. "Let me tell you about it."

There and then for the first time I heard of a restless people who centuries before had journeyed westwards in search of a land destined for them according to their seers or druids. He spoke of the Celtic federation in central Europe and its coming to Ireland equipped with a knowledge of iron, enamel, and wonder-tales. He ended his talk by saying, "Neither your teacher nor I is allowed to teach their language—and yours—in this classroom. If we do," he said, "I may again be arrested. Your teacher could be sacked. But if you would like to come after school to the library at five o'clock, I shall have a class for boys of your age."

Enquiries revealed that the man was Tomás Ó Donnchú, a zealot known later as "fear an rothair," the bicycle man, a 1916 man recently released from Frongoch or some similar place, and a committed spirit who travelled the country to revive the Irish language. Thus began my acquaintance with a remarkable man who transferred some of his idealism to me. Tomás enrolled us in Fianna Éireann; he was subsequently arrested, and the library wherein he taught us was burned by the British forces. A year or so later he returned, so physically broken that we scarcely recognised him. He resumed his classes as if nothing had happened. Nor did he speak of his period in jail. I visited him many years later when I was selected to give Óráid an Oireachtais. Much later I was privileged to open a football pitch named after him.

The rats in the old school building were brazen. Their noses could be seen twitching at lunchtime. During the Christmas holiday the bottoms of the doors were gnawed away as a consequence of rodent famine. My terrier, Tara, was the best-blooded dog in Kerry, as the contents of a cage trap were recurrently released in the muddied playground.

The sense of famine Ireland was renewed at lunchtime. Poorer boys were lined up and given cocoa and a slice of bread and jam. Later a currant bun was added. I never came to terms with this indignity. During the years of the Second World War I asked the good women who served this food to substitute soup for cocoa. I had reckoned without the legacy of history! When, after lunch, the poorer boys emerged into the playground they were greeted with cries of "Souper!" There were no takers for the soup the day following.

In the wider Ireland, the economic war saw farmers broken and veal fed to greyhounds, while on the streets the Blueshirts paraded. Mallow had proclaimed itself a commune, and the great field at the rear of the school had been taken over by a huge gathering and ploughed, to the air of a song that went:

> *The lawn, the lawn, to feed the poor*
> *And keep the famine from our door.*

The field beyond that—what is now the greater part of the town park—had also been taken over by force and allocated to a number of cowkeepers in the town, each person being entitled to graze a milch cow for his family use.

Within me, restlessness was uppermost. What was I doing here? Life was passing me by. Why not write to my well-off cousin the papal count in Philadelphia and ask him to renew the invitation he had once extended to me to go to the United States? More often than not I took refuge in books.

The authority over me was the principal teacher; above him was the parish priest, who was manager of the school, with the power of hiring and firing teachers. He rarely interfered, except perhaps in a country parish where he considered a teacher was becoming uppish.

Local, divisional and head inspectors checked our work. The local inspector dropped in, "incidentally," as it was called, to see how the work was progressing. The visit of a head inspector was an awesome experience. The hotel porter tipped off the teachers in such cases. A young teacher was on probation for a few years till he was awarded his diploma. By and large, depending on the inspector, the system gave us a certain amount of freedom to tackle an exhausting curriculum. If the principal, manager and inspector were fair, everything was bearable.

I had cause to remember my first incidental inspection. It had happened in the old temperance hall. The din of the place and the inattention due to all kinds of distractions caused me to lose my temper. One day I found myself shouting, "I would rather be piking dung than teaching you fellows!" I became aware that a tall, spare man with a bristling moustache and eyes that twinkled from behind glasses was staring at me. It was my first contact with Joseph O'Connor, my first inspector, later a fine novelist and a good friend. Joe defused the tension in my classroom by illustrating with deft strokes on the blackboard in a cartooning manner what I was trying to teach. His lesson was not lost on me. Though my gift at drawing or cartooning was limited, I tried whenever possible to enliven a lesson with visual images on the blackboard to hold the attention of the pupils.

Joseph later returned and asked me to list the last native Irish-speakers in the area. I cycled everywhere in the barony and listed about 130 with varying knowledge of the language. He then presented me with a small smoke-impregnated manuscript beautifully written in Irish script. This I still treasure.

I taught the usual list of subjects in different classes down through the years. I taught bilingually in many of the classes; like others of my fellow-teachers I saw no insurmountable barrier to progress in doing so.

Discipline was enforced with the bamboo cane, but never to excess. Noise, however, in our mansion was the bane of our life. If the downstairs school break came at a different time from ours, the noise would allow us to get no work done, nor could the teacher beneath us hear what they were saying if we released our charges. The sound of a marble dropping on the floor upstairs reverberated like rifle fire in the rooms below.

One could deduce the conditions in the home by the quality of the food the country boys brought for their lunches. In famine days Indian maize had been imported, which was ground into yellow meal. The bread made from this meal was locally called "pake." In the 1930s it was found in many a school satchel together with a bottle of milk.

Cloakroom? This consisted of two pegs in a corner of the room, on which coats were piled mountain-high. The heap of coats, in my opinion, was the obvious cause of transmission of disease and infection. We always seemed to be closed at certain times in winter because of flu. This, I considered, was an omnibus word for a variety of diseases.

Ballpoint pens and felt-tip pens, like vacuum flasks and Tupperware, were all in the future. Ink, inkwells and pens were a source of continual trouble in the classroom. A tall bottle with a tube inset in its cork contained ink made from powder. In each class a responsible boy was given the job of making the ink and cleaning and refilling the inkwells. His hands were always dyed an alarming shade of blue, which he regarded with pride as setting him apart from the other lads. The inkwells in the long benches had to be watched: any kind of horseplay led to spillages or flying spit inkballs. Nibs had to be constantly monitored; they rusted quickly and had to be discarded. Penholders with nibs attached were sharp instruments in young hands. The J pen, N pen or Waverley pen, "which came as a boon and a blessing to men," required only a handle before use. Then came the early fountain-pens, generally of the Swan brand. They were fine writing tools.

I had ink in school by day; in the afternoons I had more ink on my hands. I often helped out my good friend Bob Cuthbertson, the local printer. His shop, where I spent most of my afternoons, boasted a platen press and a flatbed, the latter surmounted by a black cat in metal. Bob kept a supply of quill pens, which were still in use in the local law offices. Many a good ballad I wrote with the same quill pens in Bob's jobbing office, then saw them printed by the thousand in broadsheet form.

The only dash of colour came in spring, when the country lads brought in armfuls of daffodils. They lit up the dingy classroom. This was the setting against which—like many teachers throughout the land—I entertained the absurd notion of establishing a centre of education in a state enjoying liberty for the first time.

My class and I were plagued with birds and insects. Crows, gulls and pigeons haunted the playground, because the boys could not be trained to put the waste food in a container. The century-old wall around the school was holed, and there were nests of wasps and birds to be found in them. An occasional stray dog foaming at the mouth ran wild through the playground, to be greeted with the cry of "chorea"—a common canine disease of that day.

What with faeces, cocoa, soup, rats, mice, crumbs, spiders, wasps, crows, gulls, and the various insects that prey on humankind—not to mention inspectors who examined the intellect, and clergy who presided over the spirit—ours was a poor example of a centre of learning. Noisy it certainly was, but not a mansion, except in Goldsmithian sarcasm.

The world outside the school was not much better at this time. The roads were rutted, and dusty lanes turned to mud in winter. The local boys wore a geansaí and trousers, with occasionally a celluloid collar, as I once did; the collar could be washed under a tap.

The passing of a motor car was an occasion to witness and celebrate, with mud flying in winter and a cloud of dust in summer. As often as not the boys were barefoot, though in winter the hobnail shoes of the boys of middle-class parents reverberated in any hollow area. The barefoot lads were consistently cracking their toes against sharp objects, so that bleeding toes were common; the boys took a delight in lifting ancient scabs and revealing pus or new skin, a masochistic pleasure indeed.

Human nature will become accustomed to almost any privation; but although in my turn I began to accept much of this as normal, there was always a part of my mind that fermented in revolt. Who was to blame? The very reverend manager, the Department of Education, the imperial legacy, the First World War, the War of Independence, the Civil War, the prevailing apathy of parents? I could not say. I kept telling myself there were better times ahead.

I was still twenty-one. In the lexicon of youth there is no such word as "impossible"!

CHAPTER TWO

S o there they were before me, merchants' sons with Little Duke shoes, poachers and sons of poachers, weavers of fiction, the cunning, the intelligent, and the dull. Sometimes the dull were cunning in certain respects and the intelligent were dull in others. The dutiful, the diligent, the ambitious, the lovable epileptic and the equally lovable Down's Syndrome child—all were there; the nervous and the fearless, the runaways, the nail-biters, the accident-prone, the superficially perfect, and the crossgrained. The "fixers," the precocious, the kickers, the chewers of putty and mortar, the thumb-suckers, the oats addicts (I had been one myself), the sensitive, the nose-bleeders, and the mitchers; the finger-fiddlers, the gifted, the unpredictable, the ungovernable, the twins indistinguishable one from the other and who swapped names to avoid the consequence of mischief; the prey-seekers, the informers, the impenetrable, the esoteric, the horse-lovers, the deaf.

After a time all grew interesting if not precious to me. If I could only plant a seed in the imagination of each one that would fructify later in each unique individual; if only I could find the gift that I sensed was latent in each one of them:

perhaps then I would have fulfilled the purpose of my being a teacher. i would receive no thanks—but that did not greatly matter. They need not even know what I had in mind. It became an obsession with me, this sense of deducing from small signals where each one's aptitude lay, even the most seemingly deprived among them (in my early teaching days about half came from homes below the poverty line; so buoyant were the children's spirits that this did not seem to bother them).

In my mind I went over the streets of the town, the countryside too, assessing the character and customs of the people. I had to identify the advantages I could count on and isolate and use what traditional attitudes and aims were of value. I had to know what would stimulate the boys and what would turn them off; above all I had to identify what would preserve a sense of wonder.

That we had a library was the result of the efforts of an enlightened local solicitor and scholar, Matthew Byrne (who first translated the history written by Pilib Ó Súilleabháin Béarra into English). The new Carnegie Library (the old one, in which we had learnt Irish in the late afternoons, had been burned by the Tans) was across the road from the school, and the pupils were encouraged to draw freely upon it.

In the early 1920s the same Black-and-Tans had also burned the flour and meal shop of one Daniel Flavin. Dan, a booklover, when he received compensation on the establishment of the new state altered his premises and gave us one of the finest bookshops in Ireland. Every town should be blessed with a bookshop like Dan's. I can still see his fingers deftly covering a book. The complete Everyman editions were placed at our disposal to buy and exchange again for sixpence, provided we kept the pages immaculate, so that even before I became a teacher

I was reading a book a day, and often reading far into the night. I recall Dan handing me a huge unbound raw-edged book, rather like a swatch of newspapers cut up in squares and hung in old-time latrines. "Read that, Sonny MacMahon," he had said, "but don't let your mother see it." It was the first edition of Joyce's *Ulysses,* imported directly from Paris. The same bookshop was visited by Seán Ó Faoláin, Frank O'Connor, George Russell, and other well-known writers.

In the townlands stretching north and west to the Shannon and south to Tralee there was a fine tradition of scholarship. The holdings were small and the families large, and the traditional escape was by education. North Kerry boasted of three university presidents at that time: O'Rahilly of Cork, Coffey of Dublin, and Kissane of Maynooth.

In the literary context mention must be made of George Fitzmaurice, that cryptic and powerful dramatist whose work breaks open only for those whose minds are close to Irish clay. Maurice Walsh of *The Quiet Man* fame needs no adulation from me; while poet Tom MacGreevy, a confidant of Joyce and Beckett in Paris and later director of the National Gallery, on his visits home to nearby Tarbert gave us a peep at the altar of world literature and art of that time. Down to the present day this writing tradition has been carried on by John B. Keane, Brendan Kennelly of Ballylongford and Trinity College, Fr Tony Gaughan, Gabriel Fitzmaurice, and others, and projected today by the well-known literary festival of Writers' Week.

Thus I could count on a tradition that implied that education was not a foreign body set down among the pupils but something that their forebears had respect for. Many of the lads were only a generation or two removed from the spoken Irish language. The vernacular of the country children attending the school was often unexpectedly rich, and the turn of phrase of boys reared with their grandparents often brought a smile to my lips. It was, as the Colum poem describes it, "as in wild earth a Grecian vase."

There was a strong seam of folklore in the locality. The people did not call it folklore, they just thought it was something ordinary and not in the least to be wondered at. This seam was there for me to explore every night in the kitchen of the local blacksmith, Dan Bunyan. That gathering constituted another kind of school where I learnt but rarely taught.

With the doors of the forge open all day, people were coming and going on various errands and leaving their news behind them. The smell of burning hooves, the rarest of smells in Ireland today, prevailed in the neighbourhood of the forge. By long tradition the smithy has been a centre of revolution. In the last century copies of the *Nation* were read out by a literate man seated upon the anvil. (In my teens, winter nights would find me at the head of the kitchen table, writing boycott notes to bailiffs with my left hand, and telling my hearers I was spelling the crucial word as "bycot" and warning them to spell it correctly if questioned.)

As a youth I was often left in charge of the forge when the smith's mealtime came around. I was always warned to let no-one take any of the forge water—the water that cooled the red-hot metal—to which much superstition was attached.

In the "rambling-house" at night, especially in winter, twenty or more men gathered and began discussing politics, telling tales, and singing songs. No song emanating from outside Ireland was allowed. Piseogs and salmon were topics regularly under discussion; most of those present were master-poachers. It was in this atmosphere I spent my nights for almost twenty years.

At first I was by far the youngest person present.

Pots of gold, fairy forts, the prophecies of Colm Cille, ghostly night riders, headless coachmen, landlords who had cursed their tenants as vermin and who in turn were plagued by vermin on their deathbed, with a servant girl using a quill to wipe the dead face clean of the crawling insects; faction fighting, half-forgotten ballads, the merits of barbed and unbarbed gaffs, herbal cures, holy and unholy wells—these were my fare night after night for a score of years.

Conscious of seanchas going to waste, I invited the great folklorist Séamus Delargy to visit our rambling-house. He brought along a cumbersome recording machine. The men were slow to start, but having started they were slower still to finish. They ranged over a great number of topics, all coming under the head of seanchas. The talk went on far into the night. When, as sober as a judge, the scholarly visitor had returned to the hotel, the more boisterous of my "classmates" proceeded to celebrate. They got into a "night pub" and later emerged to whoop, "We're the people! They came down from Dublin to record our learning." I had to round some of them up; the blacksmith had somehow got hold of the local Garda sergeant's overcoat and at three o'clock in the morning was directing non-existent traffic in a deserted street. "The Great Folklore Drunk" was how this event was referred to in later years.

I owe a great deal to the informal education the rambling-house provided. The orators there were merciless in argument. They would have no hesitation in hauling one's dead parent out of his or her grave and, so to speak, striking an adversary between the two eyes with the corpse if it was thought this ploy would score a debating point.

Take offence and one was out! "He hit the hurdles" was the racing expression used; one's exclusion was followed by a certain low-pitched mocking whistle, coming, it seemed, from nowhere. The callous debating skin I developed stood me in good stead in the lecturing outings I took on much later in the United States. I was neither fazed nor fussed when asked awkward questions.

The men among whom I spent these nights constituted a cross-section of the town and for me pointed to an almost classless society. The smith was, informally of course, Ceann Comhairle; under him were a postman, a joiner or two, a retired publican, a plumber, and a hardware merchant who had smuggled inside the barrels of farmyard pumps from England small arms for the flying column. There was a greyhound trainer, a harnessmaker, a soft drinks distributor, a fishmonger, a miller or two, a shoemaker, several turfcutters and market hands, a cowkeeper, a fowl merchant, and three or four who acknowledged themselves labourers. There were ex-soldiers, veterans of the First World War, and even one or two who had served in the Boer War. One old fellow who had served in India, the Andaman Islands and Palestine gave us pen-pictures of his experiences. The fact that many of these were the grandfathers and fathers of my pupils was of help to me if misunderstandings arose.

It has always struck me how people remain convinced that what is called a university is confined to an imposing building, usually in a city that is considered important either by size, status, or history. I continue to maintain that there are other "universities," which the eager scholar-observer may attend with profit. There is the University of the Library, latterly that of the Paperback, the University of Travel, and the University of the Common Man, in each of which the autodidact may graduate at his or her own pace and to their own satisfaction.

This prompts me to refer briefly to two other "schools" I attended: the "Dancing School," if you please, over which one of the great dancing-masters, Jerry Molyneaux, presided, and the Academy of the Market Place, over which my grandfather held sway and which was there for my ready attendance, just outside our back gate.

All the while I bore in mind that there was nothing highfalutin' about teaching. It often connotes drudgery, conformity, application, monotony, and rota. It can be nerve-sapping in the extreme, but with an unexpected sense of keen self-satisfaction occurring at the oddest moments. I had to achieve a balance. Like many another teacher in the Ireland of that hour I often stopped in mid-class and, looking at the pupils, asked myself, *"Quo vaditis, fratres?"*—Where are you to go? Were they to be scattered to the ends of the earth, sinking without trace in a foreign land? Those of affluent parents would inherit a sufficiency of comfort in their own country; the rest were invoiced for Britain or America. To teach them to be survivors, or, to use a modern expression, entrepreneurs, I had to lead, drive or coax them along the harsh road to knowledge. I could take the easy option of course, set them to playing fox and geese in class, and be accounted popular, but my conscience said no to this temptation. Above all they had to be taught how to pull themselves up by their own bootstraps.

1936 was an important year for me, as I achieved a balance in another sense. Following an introduction in Lisdoonvarna and a courtship that took me to the lush grasslands of Tipperary, I married Kitty, related to almost everyone in the South Riding of that county, and inevitably a Ryan. This I did on a salary so ridiculously low that it scarcely deserved mention. Five sons arrived in quick succession, and I now had to rummage about my extramural activities to find some way to augment my salary and thus educate my family. But my philosophy at that time was (and still is) that one is happy only when one is struggling, and that anticipation is often better than realisation.

To augment my miserly salary just before the Second World War I opened a bookshop in my wife's name on the main street, where my house was. I had also begun to write, largely for Seán Ó Faoláin in *The Bell*.

My average working day was now made up as follows. From nine to three at school, hammer and tongs, with no drawing back. From three to four I ate my dinner and slept—the nap as a result of excellent advice I had received from an old schoolmaster, who counselled me always to let the sediment of the school day settle in the well of the mind. From four to nine I assisted or relieved my wife in the bookshop. From nine to ten I walked about the streets with my lifelong friend Ned Sheehy. At ten on the dot I sat at a table and wrote until one in the morning. This routine I kept up for the better part of fifteen years, and lived to tell the tale.

At that time *The Bell* was under the editorship of Seán Ó Faoláin, with Frank O'Connor, Maurice Walsh and Peadar O'Donnell also on the board of directors. During the war years this magazine strove for openness of expression in every aspect of Irish life, and opposed the rigid system of literary censorship that then prevailed. My association with *The Bell* was viewed with suspicion by some clerical authorities—not all, I hasten to add, as some of the clergy, including some of the authorities in Maynooth, realised that a new literary movement and a broadening of attitudes was inevitable.

I had also contributed an article to a book called *The Vanishing Irish*, edited by Dr John O'Brien of the University of Notre Dame. The good professor was concerned that since the home population was falling, Irish vocations to the priesthood and consequently a dearth of missionary zeal would damage the Catholic Church throughout the world. He asked a group of Irish writers, including me, to give their opinions on the problem. "Straight from the shoulder" was the attitude he recommended when he came to visit me.

I trotted out the old stories of the clerical denunciations of "company-keeping"—this seemed to be the only sin in the Decalogue at that time—the tyranny exercised by the clergy over dances, even over crossroad dances, and the narrowness of censorship laws as regards literature.

When it was published, the book caused a furore. A Sunday newspaper serialised the articles, including my own, and I became the subject of much misunderstanding. How dare a national teacher, whose employer was the parish priest, utter such sentiments? I woke up one morning to find that I had been mentioned from at least three pulpits in the locality. I also received the traditional "belt of the crosier" from a bishop or two.

This did not bother me in the least. I was conscious of an inner sense of rectitude, and this even though I had gone so far as to say in my article that the reverend manager "who fails to ensure that the pupils entrusted to his care are educated under hygienic conditions is railing scrap-iron to the enemies of his church, which will one day be returned to him or to his successors in Christ in the form of shot and shell." That was strong language at that time.

The success with some of my publications in America, my

first collection of short stories, *The Lion Tamer*, and my first novel, *Children of the Rainbow*, resulted in a great deal of publicity for me. Back in Ireland some people in authority did not know what to make of me.

While grave events on the Continent during the war left us largely unscathed, laughter breaks out in my mind when I recall the events that followed on May Day in the year 1946. The Department of Local Government and Public Health made one of the most egregious mistakes in its honoured history. Acting in the best interests of the children, the department, through the schools, issued a momentous pamphlet, called *Louse Infestation: How to Treat It and How to Avoid It*.

The first page of this modern-day Epistle to the Unclean bore an enlarged reproduction of a louse in all its unglory. The text continued: "Your child may become infested as a result of sitting beside a verminous child or if any of his clothes are placed in contact with those of such children." The head louse, the body louse and the pubic louse were then described in detail; this was followed by information on the latest chemical discovery, DDT. The concluding paragraphs developed the theme: lice were the means by which typhus fever was spread; if a louse from an infected person got onto the body of a healthy person, typhus fever would develop and might be transmitted to other members of the family. If lice were exterminated typhus fever could not become epidemic and would quickly disappear. A timely and salutary document, and who could fault it?

However, it set the mountain of public outrage on fire. Protests came from all parts of the land. It was an insult to the children of Ireland to say that they even knew what lice were!

If two children were seated side by side, which was the prime transmitter of *Pediculus humanus capitis*? Suspicion was rife. Whispers came to me: "Don't have Johnny So-and-So sitting beside my son." It took a while for this row to blow over, only to be followed by darker clouds on the horizon when parental wrath was again aroused to fever pitch.

I had been appointed principal of one of the schools, the previous principal having died before his time, largely because of the appalling conditions under which we worked. Having contracted pneumonia, he survived only a few weeks. The principal of the adjoining school, in which I had served up to then, was unwilling to start or support any kind of protest against conditions; he was approaching pensionable age and did not want to risk an upheaval. I perfectly understood his position and his reluctance to protest. He too collapsed and died before his time.

As I pondered my predicament, a resolute man in the person of Frank Sheehy, afterwards chairman of the Munster Council of the GAA, was appointed to the adjoining principalship. He had been headmaster of an endowed school in Oldcastle in Co Meath. Although he had been a pupil of our school and, like my brother, also a monitor, he could not credit his ears, eyes and nose at the conditions prevailing when he took up his duties.

We decided on a course of action. It was a very simple one, and, despite some harrowing experiences, it proved to be successful.

Frank and I drew up a document. We had already decided that the practice of having a small group of boys, all of whom were on or just above the poverty line, clean out the vile toilets every afternoon would not be continued. What if some of these boys contracted a disease while engaged in this filthy work? We could be held responsible, as we had failed to officially inform the very reverend manager of the conditions obtaining. Any court of law might find us personally culpable. So we dispatched a letter on the following lines:

Very Reverend and Dear Manager:

As you are aware, the practice in these schools has been and still is for the poorer section of the pupils to brush the classroom floors and clean the lavatories each afternoon. When one considers that the lavatory seats are damp and as a consequence the boys do not use the toilets properly, with the result that a pile of faeces remains on the boards, you will readily appreciate our predicament. Therefore we ask you to give this matter your very urgent attention with a view to having the matter rectified.

We remain your obedient servants...

The result was a silence as of the tomb.

After a discreet delay we wrote another letter outlining our growing concern. Still no reply. Finally I drafted a long memorandum setting out the absolute impossibility of educating pupils in this type of school. There followed a detailed list of the problems.

A copy of this document signed by Frank and myself was sent to the manager and also to the bishop, requesting each of them to countersign to the effect that it was a true presentation of the facts. A third copy was sent to the County Medical Officer, and a fourth to the head office of the teachers' union, the INTO. Finally, when nothing seemed to be moving, we informed the then secretary of the INTO, Dave Kelleher, that we were stopping the cleaning of the toilets on a certain day.

The Central Executive Council of the INTO agreed to back us

in any action we would take, even if it resulted in a strike on our part. Our last letter on the matter was sent to the manager stating that we were ending our cleaning rota for the toilets and that the results would have serious repercussions in the town. We relied on him to make alternative arrangements.

In addition to this we had done something that clearly portrayed the conditions we worked under. We had asked a local photographer to take pictures of boys floundering in the winter muck, together with further unsavoury aspects of the building. These we held in reserve. Then we waited.

To his credit the bishop countersigned, confirming that our complaints were well founded; the County Medical Officer did likewise. Meanwhile the piles of faeces mounted. If the toilet was objectionable after a day, it was unbearable after a week, and incredible after a month.

The parents began to take notice. They visited the school, saw the disgusting state of affairs, and announced that they were withdrawing their children from this vile building. As staff we had no objection whatsoever. So began a strike of parents. For a while the school struggled on, until eventually the attendance was reduced to the teachers' children. The teachers continued to attend in empty classrooms, waiting for events to reach a climax.

At this point I pause to say that I am aware that this may seem a local problem, but it had its importance as a test case and as being a struggle for a school. It stood for many hundreds of substandard—to use a mild word—schools in Ireland in which hundreds or even thousands of teachers were forced to teach and which children had to attend. This, thirty or more years after the foundation of our adventurous new state!

A brave curate stepped in at this point. Calling out the fire brigade, he asked them to hose down the piles of excrement that had mounted in the cubicles. It was a memorable day in the town when the fire brigade was called out for this most unusual purpose.

A public meeting ended in fireworks. One speaker compared the reverend manager to a ship sunk at the mouth of a harbour so that no vessel could go in or out.

Eventually our document found its way to the office of the Minister for Education. A meeting in Dublin was arranged with the minister, Dick Mulcahy, to be attended by a deputation of the INTO, with Frank Sheehy and myself present.

The meeting opened formally. Our presentation lay on the table; so did the series of photographs. Our complaints were voiced and received courteously, and the meeting rambled on. Presently I began to chafe at the apparent insouciance with which the matter was being treated by the authorities, which could end with Frank and myself returning to Kerry with little achieved, the whole matter destined to rumble on in the bowels of bureaucracy.

I watched my opportunity carefully. When the sheaf of photographs was being examined, with the minister equably asking, "What have we here?" I, until then a back-room boy, broke in in Irish, saying, "I will explain, minister." Walking forward to the table, I said, "You see these mud-spattered children?" "Yes," he said. "The first boy there is a grandnephew of Michael Collins. The second boy covered in mud in the school yard is the grandson of a man who sat in the first Dáil with you and was a member of your party. Thirdly, this boy clothed in muck from head to foot is a nephew of Thomas Ashe, who, as history records, fought with you in north Dublin in the Easter Rising, a man who subsequently died as a result of forced feeding while on hunger-strike. You will bear with me, minister, if I say that these, the inheritors of your revolution, were rewarded with squalor."

I then walked back to my seat. There was silence for a moment or two. I heard the minister speak under his breath to the secretary of his department—a man for whom I had the highest regard. "Cé hé sin?" The answer, from Tarlach Ó Raifeartaigh, a fine teacher and scholar well known to us from our St Pat's days, was, "Bryan MacMahon, one of the principals; he writes a bit." The rest was inaudible, but I had the feeling that Tarlach was on our side and had probably contributed in bringing matters to a head, if not a successful conclusion.

The schools were visited afterwards by another Minister for Education, Seán Moylan, a joiner by trade and also a freedom-fighter. Seán was a gentleman, forthright too, and a man of high intellectual capacity. Taking a penknife from his pocket, he thrust the blade through the window frame, right up to the hilt. The timber was rotten to the core. He smiled, then turned to me and asked me if we wanted a library in a new school. "Not particularly," I said. "Why?" he asked. "I would prefer the children to get into the habit of going across the road to the Carnegie Library, so as to carry that habit into their teens, when they would have long left our care and direction." I did not wish library activities to be associated with a school setting.

From the day our new school was built a dynamic era began for the children of our locality. The paint-bright rooms almost blinded us with their marvellous colours; I have nothing but praise for the architect and contractor. The new manager ensured that the staff were consulted at every phase of the work. It was a lovely building, with a Séamus Murphy statue above the main doorway. The teachers and I persuaded the parents to knit multicoloured geansaís for the children. When the inspector arrived he blinked at the riot of colour before him.

I shed few tears when steel cables were tied around the upper part of the old school. For a moment or two it swayed on its foundations; the bulldozer roared with anger, thrust forward, and down the old school tumbled in a cloud of dust.

The building had been vandalised the night before by hooligans wreaking vengeance for the dark days spent therein. My efforts to track down the culprits were half-hearted, as I could understand their frustration at having to spend so many years in such an unsuitable hulk. I half-envied the vandals, as I would like to have done the same foul deed myself and purge myself of years of pain within its walls.

We entered the new building with a sense of glee and achievement. On the occasion of the production of a pageant of mine in Croke Park I buttonholed Jack Lynch, who I knew was leaving the Department of Education in a matter of weeks. I reminded him of his promise to give us an assembly hall. "I'll see to it before I leave Education." Which, as Éamon Kelly the seanchaí says, he did.

It was a joy to work in the new building. We had a public address system, if you please. A picture window afforded me a panorama of the wood, the hills, and the fields, all from my classroom table. The light could be controlled by venetian blinds. Teachers, pupils and parents relished the new atmosphere. We had airiness, lightness, and brightness.

I could now follow the wheel of the seasons through the window. In spring and early summer it was delightful to see a bare tree gradually come to life in gentle green right on the site of the old fort of Tuathal, from which Listowel takes its name. Day after day as the year advanced I watched that tree lose its green colour, then turn a pale wine-red, before becoming a marvellous copper. A pheasant laid her eggs and hatched out a clutch of young ones at the end of the school playing-field.

From 1836 to 1959 was a long period for a community to spend in scholastic inferiority—from the point of view of the building, that is. For the teachers and for me personally it meant that we could now devote all our energies to teaching. For me also it offered a breathing space in which to recall the many humorous and human incidents that lighten the tenor of the school day. For a school is nothing if it is not a place of laughter and song.

CHAPTER THREE

On John Gay's tombstone there is the following epitaph:
Life is a jest; and all things show it.
I thought so once; but now I know it.

Despite its serious aspects, a school, if it is lucky, possesses a sense of humour. Scarcely a day passed, whether under the dire conditions obtaining in the old building or in a modern staff room, without anecdotes being exchanged by the teachers.

Anyone who studies the origins of literature will find that creativity usually has its beginnings in unusual conversations and attitudes, and will also discover that, as often as not, these situations are born out of a sense of humour.

Frank O'Connor has said that the original storyteller was a Stone Age prankster who left the circle around the fire at night, went out into the darkness, possibly to relieve himself, and returned with a story that he had encountered a lion. He had thrust his hand deep into the lion's open mouth, caught its tail and turned the beast inside out—by his own version. When later the same joker stood up from his stone seat in the half-darkness and began to mime his deed to the accompaniment of joyous shouts of appreciation from the others—drama was then born.

Arthur Koestler in his memorable book *The Act of Creation* traces the transition from jester to sage to artist, explaining why the jester was the father of all literature. This transition, I found, had parallels in teaching, which I made use of to the full, often doing so intuitively in a manner that I myself dubbed as crazy ad hoc. Many years later, in conversation with former pupils, some of whom were then adults or even elderly men, they invariably recalled incidents in school that had an element of zany humour about them.

To me humour has the quality of indelibility: this quality connotes the presentation of the unusual in a usual way, or vice versa. Literature presents the novel as commonplace and the commonplace as novel. This, I reasoned, could be the foundation of something of value in the classroom as well as in the library.

In a well-made play, every sentence must convey one of three things, possibly two or all three together—that is, if the playwright is talented or lucky: every comment must advance the plot, throw light on character, or raise a laugh. This principle of the stage was something I kept constantly before me in my teaching days. How to develop it in the classroom was the question.

One such incident happened shortly after our moving into the new building. One day there was a knock on the little glass panel in the door of my classroom. Opening the door, I found a young man not much more than a boy, a stranger, standing there. He explained that he was the advance publicity man for a circus. He had a sallow skin; I took him to be an Indian or Pakistani. Very courteously he asked if I would urge the children to attend a little circus that was to visit the town the following day. The tent would be found in the usual circus spot in the field beside the river. He asked if I would be good enough to announce it over the public address system in the school.

As we walked along the corridor to the little staff room I suddenly stopped. "What acts have you got?" I asked. "We are a very small circus," he said sadly. "We have not got great international talent. But we earn a living." He was humble, even apologetic. "Have you an elephant?" I asked. "Yes," he said, "but it is a baby elephant." "How big is the elephant?" I asked. "His shoulder comes up to here," he said, extending his arm to indicate the animal's height. "Is he quiet?" "Most docile," he said. "Fine," I said. I had seen an opening for some fun. "If you want to have the town ringing with the news of your circus, do exactly as I say."

At this time I had been matching wits with the children, or pretending to. I had allowed them to score over me on a few occasions, for there is nothing dearer to children's hearts than to confound the teacher. The wise pedagogue often pretends to be in error. "Pretend you don't know, sir" is a plaint I have often heeded. The time had come for me to prove that I was not an abject idiot.

"So," I said to the circus lad, "be here tomorrow at noon on the dot. Lead your elephant in by the front gate very quietly, come down the middle of the playground to the main door here; don't let anybody see you. Lead the elephant in here; I will have opened the two doors; guide him across the corridor and stand at my classroom door at twelve o'clock exactly. If you do this I will guarantee a full house for your matinée performance, and a good attendance for the night show too." "That is very good." "We will synchronise our watches—and remember: twelve o'clock on the dot."

I knew the following day's lesson made reference to a magician. At five minutes to twelve I expanded on the word "magician" and said to the boys that I was letting them in on a very special secret. "I am a magician," I said solemnly. "I don't want everybody to know, but it happens to be true."

The class shook with laughter. One boy asked, "What can you do?"

"If I repeat a certain formula of words, any wild animal will materialise here in the classroom."

"Can you get a tiger?"

"No tigers, they are too dangerous," said another lad.

"A mouse?"

"Yes, but it's too small," I said.

"Rats?"

"Yes, but we've had enough of those already."

Someone was bound to suggest the animal I had in mind. "An elephant," one said at last.

"Certainly," I replied quickly. "I like elephants."

"Not a big one," someone suggested. "A baby one will do."

The hands of the clock stood at three minutes to twelve. Out of the corner of an eye, through the window in the classroom door, I spied my accomplice leading the little elephant across the yard and entering the school through the open door.

"We're waiting. Where's your elephant, sir?" came the cry of the impatient class.

Raising my hand for silence, I made passes in the air with my willow rod. Again out of the corner of my eye I could see the waiting mahout, dressed in Eastern garb. "Abracadabra," I chanted. "All together now to give power to the magic." All the class chanted, in varying tones of belief and mockery. "Oscail an doras," I told the boy nearest the door. "Let in the elephant."

The boy hesitated, then opened the door. He backed away in utter disbelief as in came the trunk, the head and finally the

entire baby elephant—it too was dressed for the occasion—
followed by the mahout. There was a gasp of astonishment.
Excitement then broke its bonds, and everybody began to cheer.
The elephant looked on quietly out of its tranquil eyes: it had
become used to the vagaries of circus audiences.

This incident, and later the school announcement over the
public address system, gave the little circus the publicity it had
asked for. All that week, wherever I went, I was bombarded with
questions about what on earth was happening in the school.

A teacher and a writer draw sustenance from the same reservoir
of energy; each, as it were, "prances on the front lawns of other
people's brains," and seeks to do so with the aim of indelibility.
In both my roles, as teacher and writer, I venture to stress once
again that success begins with humour.

Why does one recall a single incident above a thousand
others in a crowded life? One photograph above the hundreds
in a packed album?

Let me offer an instance of black humour, which I confess
illustrates a certain measure of shabbiness on my part. When
the school had closed for the summer holidays, I was finishing
the yearly returns in a sunlit silent classroom and idly wondering
where I would go wandering. To Clare on my bike, a latter-day
William Bulfin? To beloved Coumeenole, or to Clare Island? To
west Cork, with its almost tropical coves and groves?

There was a knock on my classroom door. An old
countrywoman stood outside. I could barely see her eye in the
fold-over of her shawl. There was something clever about the
way she looked at me. "May I have a word with you privately,
master?" she said. She came into the classroom and sat down.

"What can I do for you?" I asked.

"I'm having some Yankees to visit me, master."

"I see."

"They're very important people."

I nodded.

"I live up in the high mountain, where we have no toilet facilities. In pardon to you, we generally use the field behind the house."

"I understand."

"I hear you have a portable lavatory for the children in the infants' department across the road."

"It's called an Elsan," I said.

"I have a donkey and car in town," she said, "and I thought that maybe as the children are on holidays today you might oblige me by giving me a loan of your portable toilet for the summer."

I paused. I knew the playboy in the town who had given the woman this advice. "Of course I will," I said.

"That's a weight off my shoulders," she said with a sigh.

I'm sorry to say that I was being disingenuous and not a little unfair, as I had no intention of giving her the toilet, which was Government property. I paused and said, "Would you first go down to the church and knock at the top confession box at the left-hand side—between penitents, of course. When the canon puts out his head ask him for the form."

"What form?"

"The form you must sign when taking property from a Government building. That you'll return it safely—just a matter of routine."

"Sign for it? Ask the canon and he in the confession box?"

"He's the manager of the school. He'll be delighted to do it for you," I said. (There would be an explosion in the church if

[42]

she made such a request at such a time.)

The woman paused. "I won't bother with it." she said, "There's too much involved."

Sometimes a teacher is taken aback by a pupil's ability to probe a problem to the full and to offer answers that the teacher himself has not anticipated.

In a rudimentary science class I had begun with the following statement: "All knowledge comes to us through the senses. Seeing, hearing, smelling, tasting and touching are the five great gateways of knowledge. I am now about to give you an example of the working of each of these senses.

"Watch carefully. I now have two beakers. They look alike and contain the same level of liquid. But one liquid is water; the other is salt and water. How do we use our senses to tell which is which?"

"By tasting," all but one lad shouted. This sleepy fellow had blurted out, "By seeing." The class rewarded him with a guffaw.

"Come out," I said to the culprit. "Do you mean to tell me that by seeing you could tell which is clear water and which is salt and water?" A dull silence followed. "As a matter of fact," I added, "if you looked at those two liquids from now until the crack of doom you couldn't tell which was water and which was salt and water."

A hand shot up from the back of the class. It was a reserved lad who rarely spoke.

"Well?" I asked somewhat crankily.

Adjusting his spectacles, the scholar said, "If you looked at the beakers from now till the end of time, sir, the water in both vessels would evaporate and you would then be left with crystals at the bottom of the glass that contained the salt and water."

For me there is an element of sadness in the following incident. True, it begins with humour, but it ends in pathos.

It was two o'clock in the afternoon in the somnolent summer schoolroom and my class was inclined to doze off. So I said, "All put down your heads and sleep. In a few minutes' time, when I call you, you will make an effort to imitate some animal, bird, or reptile."

All gratefully put down their heads. Time passed; the children woke up, and they warmed to their task. One roared like a lion, one bellowed like a bull, one crowed like a cock, one whinnied like a filly, one bleated like a lamb. Growling, squawking, whistling, quacking, neighing, purring, lowing, hissing—each sound in its turn filled the air of the classroom. I was Noah in the body of the noisy ark.

When peace was restored I returned to Mícheál, a highly intelligent and dignified boy with an outlook on life far more mature than that of his classmates, who had sat motionless during our little game.

"Well, a Mhichíl," I said, "how about your mimicry of some little animal or bird?" No response. The class grew tense. I now began to realise, vaguely as yet, that I had invaded the territory of a boy's dignity. He was silently refusing to have hand, act or part in the silly proceedings. Still, in my stubbornness I reckoned I could not afford to be defied.

"I'll give you another few minutes to think of it," I said lightly. Everyone in the classroom knew that Mícheál was in revolt. Time passed, and the tension mounted. Still no sound from the young rebel.

"Son, please make some little sound," I pleaded. "I don't care how miserable it is, but please, don't defy me." No answer. It was beneath his dignity.

I was possibly suffering from end-of-the-day exhaustion and was unable to see that I was painting myself into a corner. The boy continued this state of silent revolt until three o'clock, when the bell rang to signal the end of the school day. The other children scampered off; I asked my young rebel to remain behind. "Why didn't you mimic the bird or animal as I asked?" Still no answer, even though he was usually well able to account for himself.

Okay, I told myself. I may have upset his dignity, but at this stage it was either his dignity or my discipline. I on my throne of authority, he seated in his desk, we sat facing each other in the soundless schoolroom. "You may go home only when you have learnt to obey," I said.

Having decided to sit it out, I began to correct copybooks, leaving the boy wrapped in his cocoon of silence. Every now and then I looked up and asked, "Anything yet?" The hands of the clock circled the dial; it was four o'clock. Still no answer. "Any sound at all and we can both go home happy?" Failure! I was hell-bent on seeing the bitter contest to its end. (How stupid can one get?)

I called him up to the rostrum. He came obediently. "A Mhichíl," I said, "I know everyone belonging to you. Your dad is a great friend of mine; so is your mother. Your grandfather was a schoolteacher; if a boy defied him he would be angry. Please make some sound." No answer to my emotional blackmail.

The afternoon dragged on. Four; four thirty; five; five fifteen. By this time I had the day's supply of copybooks corrected, and my patience was all but exhausted. I was still adamant, brainlessly telling myself that even if I had to remain till midnight to win the struggle I would do so; and still no sound from the boy.

I put down my head and began to write. After an agonising

pause I fancied I heard a small sound coming from among the benches. I looked up. "Was that a turkey?" I said, looking out the window. No answer. I went back to my books. Again came the sound: "pioc"—just like that. "That was excellent, a Mhichíl," I said. "Now we can both go home. Slán agus beannacht."

Mícheál died in a motor accident when he was just reaching manhood, with the prospect of a brilliant academic career just ahead of him, one that was realised to the full in the other members of his family. I learnt much from this incident. A teacher, like an army, must always have a line of retreat. Early in his career he should be able to recognise the difference between stubbornness of will and tenacity of purpose. A wise man once told me, "Many of the woes of mankind arise from three insecurities: insecure gentility, insecure scholarship, insecure authority." I recalled this advice too late. As a teacher, one continues to learn until the day of retirement.

Jody was unique. He was not interested in formal learning. He seemed always to be looking out the window as if he were anxious to get on with the business of challenging the world. He and I often fell out with each other; we fell in again just as readily. A rule I learnt from my mother was never to let a child return home with a grievance.

Jody's extraordinary energy was a disruptive factor; his strong fist was often in action. I could never see the humour of him in class; I saw it clearly when the school was over. I found myself telling stories about him then. In despair I cast about to find what he was interested in. I realised then that he had a passion for figures.

Maths at our level was rudimentary. Be that as it may, I set him the task of learning tables—addition, subtraction, multiplication, and division. We had tables competitions; he emerged the champion. When Jody had reached the 12 times multiplication tables I allowed him to go on to 13 times and even up to 19 times, a feat beyond my own ability. Finally at 29 times multiplication tables I stopped him before it could become an obsession with the boy.

"Are you really going to the United States?" I asked him one day, for a rumour to this effect had spread in school. "Yes, sir." "Father, mother, and all the family?" "Yes, sir." "Goodness me, what will we do without our mathematician?" I said, my tongue planted in my cheek.

When the day arrived for Jody to say goodbye I was genuinely sorry to see him go. He fulfilled the school rites of departure, going around to every class as he bade his last farewell. When finally he had left us, a sigh compounded of sorrow and relief rose from the entire school. We teachers did not know whether to be happy or sad at his departure.

The years went by, and, as had so often happened before, there came a knock on my classroom door. Opening it, I found an upstanding young man dressed in vivid green with a comely and obviously American young woman standing beside him.

"You don't remember me, Mr MacMahon?" he began, twanging the name as only Americans can. The face was vaguely familiar, but so far I could recall no name to match it.

"I'm Jody," he said. "Jody of the tables."

"Good Lord, Jody," I said, "I'm delighted to see you."

He introduced me to his fiancée, telling me he had come back to get married in Ireland. Here I reveal one of the rewards of a teacher's life: the meeting of one's former pupils under happier circumstances. Most of all he wanted me to attend his wedding breakfast in a Dún Laoghaire hotel. I was leaving for a booked holiday in the Canary Islands two days before the date, so there was no way I could accept; it was a minor heartbreak for me that I could not do so.

"How did you get on in the States?" I asked him later.

"Marvellous," he said. "The guys in grade school over there never learnt tables. Not like I did. The simplest sums, they had to make 'em out on paper. I had the answers in my head. You know what my teacher over there did? He sent me from class to class to solve problems in my head. A mathematical freak they called me. They put me on radio. By this time I could go up to 45 times tables. I was onto a good thing all the way from little old Listowel Boys' National School."

"What then?" I asked.

"After graduating, the teachers alerted the Bell Telephone Company, saying that I was a math genius. Having been told so many times that I was, I decided to become one. They put me through college. Now I hold down a good job with the Bell Company, and I'm still on my way up. All due to the fact that you taught me the tables."

Happy is the childhood that has a river flowing through it. Like any community with a river close by, in our town and district the lives of the schoolboys revolved around the River Feale, especially during the fishing season. I use the word "fishing" guardedly; more often than not it was the poaching of salmon or trout that occupied the minds of old and young at that time.

I recall a visit of my brother-in-law, the dignified president of an ecclesiastical college, who answered a timid knock on my front door one morning before breakfast. A boy no more than eight years of age stood outside holding a paper bag partially concealed behind his back. I knew flaxen-haired Mossie as the

Champion Trout Tickler of the Western World.

"Is Master MacMahon here?" he asked meekly, not expecting to find a priest answering his knock.

"He's shaving at the moment."

"When can I see him, Father?"

"Not immediately."

A diffident pause followed, then, "I'll wait, Father."

"If it's a message, perhaps I could give it to him for you."

"All right so," the lad said, reluctantly handing over the bag, the contents of which kept slithering around.

The priest looked inside the open bag. "What are these?" he asked.

"White trout, father."

"Where did you get them?"

"I pawed 'em, father."

"You what?"

"Pawed 'em."

"You'll have to explain that, son," replied the puzzled priest.

"When the wheel stopped," the boy blurted.

"What wheel?"

"The mill-wheel, father. The water ran away from the trout, so the trout tailed down into the shallow water."

"Yes?"

"I took off my shoes and ran my fingers up under the green weed until I found a trout."

"Yes?"

"I found his gills, tickling him all the time—you understand?"

"I do."

"All of a sudden I squeezed. Then I pinned him against the bed of the stream." He illustrated the process.

"What then?"

"I gripped his gills good, brought gravel, weed and all and thrun him up on the bank."

"Is that how you tickle trout?"

"We call it pawing, father."

"I see. What am I to do with these trout?"

"Give them to Master MacMahon and tell him not to say much about them."

"All right, son, I'll deliver your message."

To my brother-in-law I could only say, "I know civil law; you know canon law; that child responds to the natural law. We'll say no more." On reaching school my young friend looked at me. I winked. He smiled.

Law-abiding citizens may view my "aiding and abetting" of poaching with horror. Let me defend myself. At the same time that these boys were being pursued for the tickling of a trout or two, an act of skill if ever there was one, local landlords, relying on a medieval ordinance, were hauling hundreds of salmon each day out of the same pools simply by netting them. To me salmon were *ferae naturae*, and bore no owner's brand.

The day of the horse fair is still a colourful occasion in the life of our small town. On such a day a red-haired pupil in my class repeatedly requested leave to go to the toilet. I did not wish to embarrass the boy by questioning him on his many excursions, suspecting a dose of diarrhoea or a complaint of that nature. Nevertheless, on glancing out an upper window I saw that the lad was standing below at the school gate, peering through the iron bars and giving instructions to a low-sized man wearing jodhpurs.

"What is he up to?" I asked the class.

"He's buying a pony, sir. He's already saved up and bought

a common car; now he's going to buy a small horse or pony with more money he's spared."

I continued to watch as several animals were trotted up and down for the boy's scrutiny. At last, amid much loud talk, a bargain was struck, spit-wet palm slammed on palm, and a roll of notes passed over—all through the bars of the school gate, during school hours.

When the boy came in, I said, "Why didn't you tell me you were buying a pony, and I would have allowed you out onto the footpath?"

"I was afraid you wouldn't let me, sir."

"What will you do with him?"

"All sorts of work. Draw sand, manure, turf, old mortar and bricks—anything."

"I hope you make lots of money with him," I said. Which later he did, and continues to do until the present day.

Life is a jest; and all things show it. I still hear the voices from across the years. "I pawed 'em, Father." "Abracadabra...let in the elephant." "By seeing." "Buying a pony, sir." "A portable lavatory." And then the sound of "pioc" in an almost empty classroom.

CHAPTER FOUR

I f there is one factor common to all school subjects it is that of reading: the interpreting of cyphers on a page, a process that constitutes a mystery for the child. The pupil must be lured to enter the mystery, to explore this magic cave, before he can unlock the secrets of the world about him. Together with many of my fellow-teachers I identify reading as the most important activity of the school day. Given the gift of reading, the child can solve from his own resources many of the problems that confront him in life and also find it a source of almost unending pleasure. The greatest intellectual disadvantage that anyone can carry through life is the inability to read.

Beyond the almost physical craft of reading there lies the appreciation of the subject-matter, and beyond that lies the love of reading, which with luck extends into the adult life of the student. That reading is a common aspect of every subject on the curriculum is something that needs to be re-stressed. From facility in reading springs a love of writing, with its embodiment of a personal creativity, and, again with luck, an appreciation of such ancillary aesthetics as poetry and song.

My long-term or horizon aim was, say, to cultivate the ability to read the newspapers thoroughly, to know how to analyse and assess what is read, and, perhaps with a tinge of scepticism, to become equipped to resist idiocy, special pleading, jargon, and manipulation. Above all I continued to ask myself whether the child as an adult would use the bookshop or public library and become a lover of books.

What follows is an example of my individual idiosyncrasy in the teaching of reading. In the course of an English lesson I had stopped suddenly and looked into space: the class watched me in perplexity. I moved behind the old blackboard; then, taking out a small red notebook from my inside pocket, and making sure I was still being watched, I began to write in it. The class was mystified. What was he up to now? What did this antic mean? I emerged and continued with the lesson.

After a while, having encountered another unusual word in the text, I repeated the procedure. Curiosity got the better of one of the pupils. "What are you doing behind the blackboard, sir?" he asked. "That's a secret," I said. I am pressed to reveal my secret. "If you are good, I will reveal the secret tomorrow," I said.

The following day at reading time I am reminded of my promise. "Some of you collect stamps, conkers, or bottle tops," I say quietly. "I collect difficult words. I keep a small red notebook into which I enter those words each day. If I don't know the meaning of a word I look it up in a dictionary."

All children have a collection mania, and this revelation appeals to those of nine or ten years of age. "Can we collect words?" they ask.

"You are much too young," I reply.

Comes a chorus of protesting voices.

"I still think you are too young," I insist.

"No, no!"

"Oh, well, tomorrow, as a special favour, I will allow the six best boys in reading to collect words in these small red notebooks that I have on my table..."

With the gentle nursing of rivalry in a wholesome way, the fever for collecting words reaches a high pitch over the next few days. By this time all boys have been issued with a small red notebook. It dominates almost every moment of the children's day. Unusual words are ferreted out.

Mild quarrels begin about who has most words. Some of the collections went into thousands of words—even the weakest boy in the class had a small hoard, which the better pupils were not only able to get him to spell but whose meaning, by some alchemy quite beyond me, had been conveyed roughly to him. I was riding on the crest of a wave.

As a follow-up to this method—call it the small red notebook or Tom Sawyer method—on our moving into the new school I allowed boys to write their difficult words in coloured chalk on the wall-to-wall felt blackboard before class proper began in the morning. They queued up to be first to enter the classroom. Soon the blackboard was a surrealist montage of words collected from all quarters and sources, from radio, television, newspapers, magazines, bottles, even shop windows. In a short time the pupils had an extensive vocabulary, which, though a trifle incoherent as yet, was a firm foundation for the reading process. Each boy learnt to use a dictionary and even to make a little dictionary of his own.

There were times when I came to realise that Diogenes was right. When the king asked how best he could serve the sage, the reply from Diogenes was, "Keep out of my light and let me see the sun." We teachers often over-teach. At times we

underestimate the intelligence of the pupils entrusted to our care.

I was happy finding the world opening before my young scholars. Largely of their own volition they experienced vicariously the cold of igloos, ventured onto the hot lava of volcanoes, tiptoed into the cave of Androcles, lolled in the groves of Tír na nÓg, rolled the stone uphill with Sisyphus, clambered up the Great Wall of China, galloped with Galloping Hogan, smoked peace pipes with Sitting Bull; and later still, I dare say, their children walked on the moon with Armstrong. Again I stress that, as is true of the writer, everything is grist to the teacher's mill: every new scrap of knowledge is an exciting experience for the child, and a pleasure for the teacher who transfers it.

Alas! There still remained a small residue of boys who couldn't read. Nowadays they would be labelled dyslexic. The word "dyslexia" is bandied about these days; for me it is a jargon word used by lazy educationalists or superficial commentators. While I do not suggest that such a state does not exist, I contend that it applies only to a small minority of pupils.

I was aware, of course, that in Ireland some children did leave school unable to read; in the general opinion of that time these were hopeless cases. And yet, observing any of these same lads at play, one was often confronted with a personality different from that displayed in the classroom. Illiteracy was not uncommon in the Ireland of fifty years ago; the semi-open voting of illiterates, a recurrent phenomenon in the polling booth, was widely interpreted as an early straw in the electoral wind, as well as being an unfavourable comment on poor attendance at school.

I set about investigating the matter in a very limited way. My day was already full and crowded. I recalled the traces of the variegated vocabulary already gleaned even by some of the laggards in the Tom Sawyer exercise, to give me and them encouragement. Behold me then in an empty classroom, baiting a trap, not for rats (as I so often did in the old ramshackle building that parodied the name of school) but for slow readers in an effort to lure them to the glory of the printed word.

I select the most colourful picture books the county library can offer. I throw the books on the floor, hide them in the corners of the room, pile them on the desk, leaving a page or two open at its most attractive spread, but in a manner that suggests that the books have fallen haphazardly and that it is of no moment to me whether they are tidied or not. I bid the selected lads to go to the room, saying that I will join them presently.

I leave a decent interval before taking with me a large roll-book, which will offer the excuse that I am otherwise engaged. I find that only one or two boys have nibbled; these drop the books from their hands as I enter, as if they have been caught redhanded in something culpable. One boy has made an effort to tidy the mess. I pretend to take no notice.

It takes quite a while for the mice to accept the presence of the cat. Still pretending to be preoccupied, I engage them in sporadic conversation. "Peter, did your father kill any salmon yet?" or "Joe, was that your Uncle Paddy I saw home from England?"

The boys answer as if their minds are elsewhere: they now have the books in their hands and are clustered round the boy who, by their standards, can make some kind of an attempt to read. I leave the room. On my return I still make no mention of the books, but note with interest that almost every boy is turning pages. Again I cut off this activity so as to reinforce the notion that I am indifferent to the subject of reading. This process might take a week of short periods every day.

The tendency to crowd around one of their number has given me the clue to my next step. "If I sent along a big boy to tell you about the books—whom would you choose?" They name boys from the senior class with whom they have some bond of admiration or affinity. Some are among the last boys in the world I would have selected. The teachers in the adjoining school kindly release my would-be assistants. Together each pair sets to work with zest.

Watching covertly and despite a mounting hubbub, I was amazed how the problem readers responded to this type of stimulus. The laggards were transformed, and made progress in a manner I did not believe possible. The tutors too, all of whom had previously been pupils of mine, underwent a metamorphosis of dignity and responsibility. Bribery on a minor scale followed.

I often found it worth while having a word with a slow learner's elder sister, if he had one, meeting her on the street perhaps and saying, "Paddy would make great progress if you gave him a little attention." It often worked!

Was I at journey's end? Not yet. I was still left with three of the original eight or nine, a trio who still rewarded most of my efforts with a blank stare. I felt inclined to leave them to their fate, but was pulled up short before I could do so.

In the course of our training as teachers we had always been counselled to observe children at play and discover their passion. Feeding this special interest—football, for example, or nature— with suitable colourful books often worked wonders. Secretly I often shouted, "Eureka! I have him!" as the tumblers of the boy's mind fell into place.

Having exhausted all my tricks over the school year, I

reluctantly had to admit that the remaining pupil or two were indeed cases of what is now called dyslexia. The rest had started on the reading process.

All of this is by way of introduction to my own idiosyncratic method in the teaching of reading. I concede that it is an experiment on a limited scale. The thrust with the main body of pupils in all the classes continues in a more normal manner. Where a problem is identified, nowadays the procedure is to allocate the work to remedial teachers, who possess a special aptitude and training for this kind of teaching.

Lest it should be thought otherwise, I stress that there is a technique involved in the teaching of a reading lesson. I learnt this sixty years ago, and it abides with me to the present day. Nowadays, with the mechanical aids available to a school, it may be reckoned archaic and even amusing. I do know that at a later stage in my career I outlined the method to young teachers from the United States; they accepted it eagerly: one wrote to me later to tell me that she had my lesson headings boldly printed on a piece of board and placed on her desk. There they remained until such time as she had mastered the method.

Again, the DIY parent may find them of some interest. It may be that they are still relevant for a normal middle class in a national school.

First there is the *arousal of interest* the day before the lesson is taught, so that the pupil is primed to read for himself. A brief informal *introduction* before the lesson begins—again to heighten interest in the text—is followed, first by the examination of *matter expressed* in the text, and then by *matter implied*. This last can be a most rewarding exercise, and children look forward eagerly to it. *Difficult words* can then be written on the blackboard, with some comment about difficulty in spelling. The teacher's *model reading* is followed at times by individual *pupil's reading*— aloud or silently. Phrases may be isolated for *composition usage* or for fantasy and fun. An informed *organic chat* (by this I mean that the hoity-toity school tone is abandoned in favour of an everyday conversational approach) could well be followed by *dramatisation of the text,* especially where there is a lively dialogue. *Committal to rote* is not to be scorned on special occasions.

This indicates in barest outline a process that for me has stood the test of time, but which may need modern modification. There is nothing rigid about it: each teacher—or parent—can use or discard some of the steps to suit the individual learner.

The final aim of that particular school year is to ensure that the pupils read ahead of the teacher; they are then questioned closely on the text. This means that many of the outlined steps can be dispensed with.

I was once asked to write a verse for a bookmark. Here it is:

The Voice of the Book

In very truth I am your friend.
I bring you sweet companionship
When all your earthly friends have fled
And kin begins to tire.
Please do not dog-ear me
Nor yet in thoughtlessness
Leave me disintegrate and die
Beside a blazing fire.

My entire life, both inside and outside the school, has been bound by stories. The oral story was, and still is, an artistic and social art, grace, or gift. It is also a useful educational tool. To this day, wherever I go, someone stops me and begins with, "I'll tell you a good one." Ninety-nine out of every hundred of these "good ones" are mere anecdotes; the precious one left is the seed of a literary story.

Here and now I am concerned with the story as an instrument of education. I am also concerned with the nurturing and fusing of story-love as it exists among the ordinary people with the story-love that manifests itself in every moment of the teacher's life, and hopefully in that of the pupils. Every facet of classroom life, every subject, even one as sober as arithmetic, can be adroitly turned into a story. To do so is the essence of the teacher's trade.

In the rambling-house of my adolescence and young manhood, anecdotes and stories—what are known in Irish as "seanchas"—fused with every stone of my country town, with every hill and hollow of the surrounding countryside, with every drop of water in my river, with every cavern on the nearby coast.

There are three great hungers in the human being: the hunger of the body, the hunger of the spirit, and the hunger of the mind. The hunger of the body is appeased by food and physical activity, while the hunger of the spirit is appeased to some extent by the endeavour to solve the mystery of human existence and to probe what lies beyond. The hunger of the mind, of the imagination, is so ethereal as almost to defy definition, but it commonly indicates its presence in the story. The common cry of children is "Tell us a story."

This tripartite life I airily call the "Three-legged stool of existence." When all three legs—the physical, the spiritual, and the imaginative—are on a proper level and I seat myself upon it, and when all three hungers seem appeased, a happiness close to tears often overcomes me. A one-legged stool or a two-legged stool causes one to fall sidelong.

I count myself privileged to have seen the last of the seanchaithe. As lads we had scant respect for the old fellow: ignorant youths as we were, we often "clodded" him, pelting him with small knobs of peat or turf. Yet when he sat down and spread his fingers above a blazing fire so that the writhing shadows were cast upwards on the whitewashed walls of his kitchen, he silenced us. Then we children were off into the magic territory of indigenous imagination.

If the boys in my class had worked diligently through the day, for the final ten minutes of the afternoon session I would dole out this old tale in episodes designed to make the story last for a full month of schooldays. I would always preface the telling of the story by saying, "With some of your grandfathers, when we were children together, I heard this story in a cabin in Gleann an Phúca, so I'm only giving back to you what is really your own."

Even today the priceless work of the Irish Folklore Commission has yet to be seen in its true perspective. Preposterous as the claim of the old storyteller to be kin to Mary Pickford then seemed—and it is small wonder that people laughed when I mentioned it—the laugh was on the other side of their faces when Mary Pickford herself turned up at St Mary's Church in Listowel in a fruitless effort to trace her ancestors, the Hennessys. Griffith's Valuation of 1852 does give a Pickford dwelling in Gleann an Phúca. This unexpected connection illustrates one characteristic of the literary short story, which I use to a considerable extent and which to some extent has dominated my life, namely the reconciliation of disparates. Preserving a "window of wonder" was a plea for the imagination in the modern world of television and "star wars" technology. This was a task I set myself.

As I wander aimlessly in south-west Kerry someone tells me that near Staigue Fort, that most impressive of stone ring-forts, there lived a man who is both a storyteller and a "character." Leaping over a stone wall close to the terraced rampart of the fort, I approach this old man, whose name is Batty O'Shea and who is now saving hay. I have never seen him before. A hayfork stuck in the ground I take in hand, as did William Bulfin many years before, and without any introduction I set to work. For some time the old fellow and I work on without speaking.

About four o'clock in the afternoon the man's two daughters arrive with a gallon of tea and some home-baked bread. I am invited to sit at the foot of a haycock and take part in the meal.

Afterwards, with small urging on my part, the old man begins to tell story after story, finally ending his performance with a smile as he says, "I make 'em up for a bit of fun and to pass away the time."

A new woodwork teacher at the local technical school has just joined us in Listowel Drama Group. "This should interest you," I say. Later we travel south-west to meet the storyteller Batt O'Shea, who lived on the Ring of Kerry coast at a place called the Black Shop.

When we find the storyteller in the local pub, a joker winks at me and then introduces me to Batty as a Polish soldier who has seen service on the western front. He adds that I am the champion darts player of Poland—Batty is the local champion—and that I have come to challenge him for the championship of Europe.

The plan advances step by step at the quiet suggestions of the laughing countrymen who throng the pub. Batty either fails to recognise me or pretends not to do so. The challenge assumes a reality, to the accompaniment of sporadic cheers for Batty or, rather feebly, for myself. Small bets are laid on the outcome of the game. We begin to play.

Early in the competition Batty establishes a firm lead; amid tense excitement, I draw level, but, rallying all his forces, the old man pulls ahead to score a narrow victory. Amid roof-raising huzzas Bartholomew O'Shea of the Black Shop is acclaimed darts champion of Europe, if not of the world.

Éamon Kelly—for he was the woodwork teacher—and I spent that night in Batty's house storytelling and singing traditional songs in Irish and English. The storyteller, his wife and their daughter play their part. Towards morning I have adroitly booked the only spare bed—a single one; Éamon sleeps on a shakedown on the landing.

The hospitable family boiled twelve eggs for our breakfast. It was a night of wonderful company and of typical Irish hospitality.

The following week was Christmas week. Éamon dropped into my house before going home for his holidays. My five sons, children at the time, their baths over and wearing only their pyjamas, squatted in front of the parlour fire. "Try one of the stories on them," I said to Éamon. He spread his fingers and began, "In my father's time..." The children watched the storyteller's lips as if every syllable were precious.

So was revived, renewed and polished the ancient craft of storytelling in Ireland. Éamon added something else to the art: he created a new form of indigenous humour on the stage; up to this we had been dependent on the West End variety, which was ill suited to our temperament.

Years later Éamon and I were together with other Irish representatives in St John's, Newfoundland; he was telling his stories in a thronged hall in the university, I was lecturing on Peig Sayers and the Blasket Islands. In the audience I noticed a group of young Inuit or "Eskimos," surely the first of their race to attend university. They were gazing up at the stage in wide-eyed wonder as if Éamon had descended from outer space. Suddenly on a throwaway phrase or gesture on Éamon's part the Inuit group fell apart in uncontrolled laughter; probably some old Inuit of their acquaintance resembled the character Éamon was portraying. The Irish art of storytelling was seen to transcend the boundaries of tribe, time, and space.

Even the dramatic narration of the simplest incident can prove to be a story for a child. Children should be lured into the who, why, when, where and how of the passing day. Their questions should be answered patiently and in an adult fashion. It does not matter how banal or superficial a subject seems to the adult, because he has experienced it a thousand times: to the child it is knowledge, and possibly introduces him to something he has never experienced.

The simplest journey on my part can later form the basis of a geography, history or folklore lesson. The description, say, of a trip to Galway from the moment that I had my breakfast can be expanded to incorporate everything from morning porridge and the merits of brown bread to waiting on the bus, the experience of a town waking up, the early Mass-goers, the milk collection, fellow-travellers, passengers going to the airport—all can be teased out to help children experience in advance the real world ahead. And all the time it is expanding the imagination. The story is everything, and everything is the story.

But I have no intention of becoming a penny-in-the-slot machine as far as stories are concerned. At times I fool the children in order to prove that I am unpredictable, to verify that I am human, with all the faults and virtues that entails. Neither do I butter pupils up: to hold their attention I change moods. Woe betide the teacher whose moods and moves can be predicted by his pupils! He's certain to be outfoxed.

About this time too, possibly because of a seminal anecdote by the south-west Kerry storyteller, I invented a character called Patsy-O, an impish boy who had five wonderful pets. I had tried out some of these stories on the pupils in school or in the garden of my son's house, surrounded by my grandchildren and their friends on the occasion of a birthday party.

There is a clear difference between the "told" story and the printed version of it. The printed version can be referred to, its future and its past, by flicking over the pages, whereas the oral story must be captured as it flies. The average child is on a voyage of discovery, intent on creating a new world for himself. The story often unlocks the door to his imagination, leading him forward to the delights of the learning process.

This leads me to the often-debated question of congenital intelligence as opposed to home environment in a child's development. Does a child of average intelligence with an educationally congenial home environment outshine one with a higher intelligence quotient but whose home (or neighbourhood) conditions leave much to be desired? I incline to the view that the home environment is more important than it is given credit for. But the matter bristles with imponderables.

Almost in spite of myself I remember the little folk tale that illustrates a similar problem and its questionable solution. A pair of gentlemen once argued the age-old question: "Cé acu is treise, dúchas nó oiliúint?" Which is the stronger, nature or formal training? The man who vouched for training as the stronger force invited his friends, including his opponent, to his house for a card game. The light for the game was provided by the host's cat, which, sitting on its haunches on the table, held erect a lighted candle. "Training," he said as he smiled, "is more powerful than nature." His opponent was more than equal to the challenge. Opening a matchbox he released a mouse; whereupon the cat dropped the candle and chased the mouse.

The foregoing discussion deals mainly with motivation, embellishment and entertainment during the school hours. But the harsh, rhythmic slog goes on. There is no royal road to learning.

Much depends of course on one's definition of education. It certainly is not always a question of finding the factors of a quadratic equation. I recall an old schoolteacher saying that the not-so-bright children in his class comforted him. "If they are all geniuses," he used to say, "who will then bring the parcels from the train?"

CHAPTER FIVE

Did I ever tire of small-town life? In the immortal words of Eliza Doolittle, "Not bloody likely!" I came to know almost everything that happened in every house, in every shop as I came and went during the day—and indeed, as an addicted walker, far into the night as well. Houses and occupants became part of the fabric of my life. There was the old film-obsessed Irish-speaker who never ceased talking about Douglas Fairbanks and Gloria Swanson; the elderly shop assistant who every morning at nine polished the long brass bar that protected the outside of the tavern window; the erudite publican who made sarcastic clerihews; and a second vintner who, the instant he saw me approaching, slid his fingers along the watch-chain that hung on the protuberance of his belly and then, cupping his turnip of a watch in his palm, checked my time of arrival at, or departure from, school.

These were the streets of my boyhood on which a district inspector of the RIC had been shot dead on 19 January 1921. The barracks whence the doomed inspector had emerged and which later was the scene of an RIC mutiny still stood. I had seen a nearby shop set alight as a reprisal for the shooting; the portly and kind professor who owned it was handed an income tax demand headed *On His Majesty's Service* a bare second before the whiskey bottles in his blazing study exploded in the flames.

There was a pub adorned with a lion and a harp above the door, the work of a highly individualistic plasterer named McAuliffe. I can still experience the rising smell from the huge barm bracks in the window of the Bridewell Bakery, and can recall the dark figure of the shoemaker seated behind his open window, his candle alight beside him and his tongue curled about one of the large ice-cream cones his pupil grandson sometimes brought him on the way home for lunch. As I came and went I greeted my friend the harnessmaker and waved to a dear friend, a retired librarian who knew more about the literary and political Dublin of the 1920s than anyone alive.

As the school lay on the roadside at the entrance to the town, I always had a number of visitors, ranging from the literary and academic to the freedom-lovers of the Irish roads.

I have a thing about tramps. Somewhere I have written that a person has as many coats as an onion, and when all are peeled off there is only left the tramp or the tinker. Every man who goes on the road has some secret reason, though he may not admit it to himself, why he left home and came to live a vagrant life, one of immense hardship in wintertime—though many wanderers hole up in country cottages or "spikes" during this period.

Among the wanderers was one Francis Kendall-Husband, a Cornish man whose red hair had moved inexorably from copper to grey with the passing of the years. He called himself the King of the World's Tramps. When he came to visit me I would take the opportunity to allow the children to experience education in a wider sense, and would conduct him with some dignity to the classroom, seat him on a chair on the little dais, and introduce him as Professor Francis Kendall-Husband TOSF. (I did not explain that the initials stood for Third Order of St Francis.) I would then tell the children that each of them was to bring a shilling after lunch, when the professor would give a recital on the harmonica. (I always said harmonica, not mouth organ.) This Francis gave to perfection—classical piece after classical piece was played. When he was leaving I would give him the three pounds or so—a considerable sum in those days—with a little extra from myself. On receiving it he would look from the money to me and back again, and then say, "Hmph, it will do for the present."

I once had a merry adventure with him in a hotel in lovely Glenbeigh in south-west Kerry, where I was passing the night building up reserves for the three-day ordeal of Puck Fair, which was to open on the morrow. Who should present himself at the door of this rather exclusive hotel but the bold Francis, seeking me out by calling my name aloud. The English guests were disconcerted to see this red-bearded tramp hold court in the bar, where he was generously plied with food and drink.

At two in the morning, when he was in the full oratorical flight of reminiscence and anecdote, some eminent lawyers staying at the hotel placed an old retired schoolmaster on an improvised bench to act as judge and, appointing real barristers who were staying as guests to defend and prosecute, formally tried Francis to determine whether or not he was happy with his life on the road.

A jury was empanelled; and what started as a comic event turned into a serious debate on the merits of a sober, sedentary post of duty as contrasted with the philosophy of a tramp who claimed to be free and happy at the same time. When the jury retired and eventually returned about three in the morning their verdict was that Francis Kendall-Husband was indeed the happiest of men. There followed a rousing cheer that brought the sleepy management to the door of the taproom, asking us one and all to lower our voices lest the Gardaí arrive to investigate the proceedings of the long-past-midnight court.

I have reason to believe that one of the wandering fraternity, a self-educated man who told me he had often slept with the Widow Green—the road edge—was the original tramp who set a gentle trap for William Butler Yeats.

"With a shafe of ballads in me hand," he said, "I lay in wait for the poet outside Gort in the County Galway. I knew he would never pass a ballad singer. When he asked me what kind of songs I sold, I answered, 'Mr Yeats, there is a power of trason in these songs!'

"I spent that afternoon as a guest in Coole, the residence of Lady Gregory. On the lawn before I left I recited 'The Lake Isle of Inisfree.' Then I bowed and said, 'Mr Yeats, you are supreme in the world of poets and mystics.' This compliment pleased him, so I went upon me way replenished with cash and whiskey."

On fair-days we had regular visits from farmers whose cattle or sheepdogs had strayed. These men headed straight for the school seeking information on the whereabouts of their animals. Word was invariably forthcoming. One should never underestimate the observation powers of some four hundred pairs of young eyes moving through the town or countryside in the early morning. Nothing escapes their attention; as teachers, we provided a clearing house for much useful and useless information. Not that we ever looked for it, but we were well informed of the comings and goings, the celebrations and sadnesses in the homes the children had just left.

I can still see the look of amazement on the face of a farmer who had lost four bullocks and was describing them in detail to me in the staff room. I had forgotten to switch off the public address system, so our conversation was being relayed into each classroom. A knock on the door revealed a timid pupil to say that the animals had strayed to the river bank, where the boy had been fishing before coming into school. Many years later the same puzzled farmer asked me how I had conveyed his request to the children!

It was a regular event for one local man, a joker, to walk in the door and thunder, "A complaint, master!"

"Is that so?" I would meekly reply.

"My eldest boy is a scoundrel."

"Tck-tck," from me.

"No tck-tck, master; don't spare him. You'll get no complaint from his mother or myself. Even if you break his back."

"Dear, dear," I'd say.

"I was coming up the street the other day, and do you know what he said when he saw me comin'?"

"No." The children would look up in perplexity and concern.

"He said, 'Look at my oul' fella.' Isn't it terrible that parental control is a thing of the past?" His voice was raised as he added, "Give him the wattle, hot and heavy. If you don't, I will, and if I start I'm not able to stop." With this final shot he would slam the school door and be gone.

This man was not married, and had no children to my knowledge. A few of the boys in the class were aware of this fact, and when the visitor had gone the whispering heads would reassure frightened faces. I would feign indignation at having been fooled.

One of the deranged, God love them all, would burst in the classroom door and, glaring at the boys, would shout, "Biddy with the timber diddy, the bastar's are callin' me that." It took me some time to pacify her. Looking out through the school window I would see a figure moving among the crosses of the adjacent churchyard. The old woman's raised voice would reach me in fitful snatches. Standing in front of a headstone with a woman's name on it she would shout, "I still have my maidenhead. Ha-ha, you bitch, what about yours?"

One incident I recall clearly, for it illustrates a principle associated with the stage. At its core is the suspension of belief: for me it also underlines the point that a play should not be overcerebral or intelligent. There is much to be said for the maxim "Drama is dialogue tied to the heels of action." This I learnt to my cost in my other capacity as a playwright.

Strolling players visited the school at least twice a year. These drop-outs from the legitimate stage or the fit-ups travelled the back roads of Ireland, especially during the winter. Moving from school to school, they put on little shows. A visit to the school a day before the event was essential to remind the pupils to bring the small entrance fee on the morrow: a shilling from each of two hundred students—in all, ten pounds, at that time a most satisfactory sum. These actors were versatile. Conjuring, card tricks, contortions, paper tearing, comedy patter or playlets in period costume came easily to them. They were a revelation to children reared on a diet of radio or television.

A gong sounded. On the makeshift platform the actor-manager, dressed in an old dinner jacket, came on stage and declared that the house in which he stood was haunted. All he had to do to inherit his uncle's millions was to stay in the house for a night, this being a condition of his uncle's will.

Darkness now descended on the impromptu stage, where the actor had seated himself and was calmly reading a newspaper. There were weird offstage moans. Taking no notice, the nephew read on.

I was seated at the back of the room, which by now held two hundred very young children. I was busily catching up on the correction of copybooks when I sensed an unusual atmosphere. I found the surface of my flesh had begun to crawl. A seventh sense told me that some of the younger children were about to become hysterical. The appearance of a shrouded, moaning figure advancing behind the man in the chair raised the tension several notches. "The ghost!" the children gasped.

They shouted to warn the nephew, who said, "What? What?" despite moans and more of the ghost. When at last the nephew looked around the spirit had vanished off stage. "No ghost!" he said scornfully.

The next time the ghost appeared she placed her forefinger to her lips to silence the babble of warning voices. She then produced a cigarette lighter and set the end of the newspaper on fire! Amid screams of warning the nephew continued to read. I sensed danger from the flames, and hysteria from the children. I stood up and walked forward to where the children could see me. The hall erupted with excitement as the man leaped from his chair to cope with the blazing newspaper. It fell to the floor from the little stage. Betraying the least concern I could muster, I trampled it underfoot. The moment of danger passed.

Shakespeare was no stranger to the Irish backwoods. I refer, of course, to the regular visits of Mícheál Mac Liammóir to the local hall, and in later years to Denis Franks, who had a wonderful collection of stories having to do with his peripatetic presentation of dramatic readings. Whenever he interpreted excerpts from *Romeo and Juliet* in a convent school, particularly the balcony scene, he always had a wonderful reaction from the senior girls.

One reverend mother, determined to get full value for the fee paid, even when the little school hall was already crammed full, insisted on trotting in class after class of infants to hear the lecture. During the most amorous part of the balcony scene a trail of children would begin to shuttle to and from the lavatory. Pausing in his interpretation of the ecstatic lover, Denis once said, "Dear reverend mother and sisters, when once again I visit you to present this most intimate scene from Shakespeare, kindly ensure that the infants' bladders are empty."

Memory too throws up a phrase from a roustabout possessed of an odd dignity, who had come to our school to get publicity for a broken-down road show. As he was speaking to me he was obviously caught by a call of nature; looking at me full in the face he said, "Schoolmaster, in this institution what are your bowel arrangements?"

The benefits our young scholars derived from such performances is debatable, yet it was exposure to a form of excellence, and years later it helped them to identify with the same talent on the boards of professional theatres.

In the earlier part of my teaching days in the bad black building the visit of the dentist had to be endured to be believed. In later years the children were sent to the dentist's surgery, and this was certainly a huge change for the better. I still cannot forget the pan of blood of the old days, placed on a chair at the side of the crowded classroom, where the lesson went ahead while the brave little patient fought his fear of the forceps that extracted his rotten tooth in the sidelong and terrified view of the class.

Now and again one of the watching children slewed off the bench and was taken out in a dead faint. A scene straight out of Dickensian England; yet no-one seemed to think it odd.

I had witnessed similar scenes in the neighbouring marketplace of my youth: the "black doctor" holding aloft a bloody molar that he had extracted with his powerful fingers from a farmer's jawbone, while a ring of country folk gaped their approval.

As well as catering for the physical health of the pupils, which improved considerably in our new surroundings, the welcome psychological service began—tentatively at first—to which pupils agitated, nervous or even battered were to be referred. Parental sensitivities had to be taken into account. The excuse offered to parents was—recall that this was a beginning— that the doctor was to examine the children's teeth or eyes. In this regard the teacher took a chance and at times was left in a peculiar position: he or she knew that in the case of certain children help was urgently needed but parental permission was doubtful. If nothing serious was diagnosed the matter could be dropped. If help was called for, each case could be handled on a personal level and at times in a roundabout way, through understanding neighbours for example.

This little deception had its smiling sideshows. One day, after mulling over the problem, I despatched to the office some boys who I considered needed help. As the boys had queued up in the corridor just outside the teachers' toilet, in which I happened to be at the time, I could not help overhearing their remarks.

"What are we here for?" one pupil asked the boy next to

him. "She wants to find out if we're crazy, you fool," came the ready reply. Another little fellow chirped up, "If there's a nurse inside, I'm not going to let her handle my mickie." This reference to the incipient organ of his manhood was natural and without prurience.

Teachers, even to the present day, are forever coping with people seeking to promote business interests, or the welfare of associations, through the unpaid agency of teachers and pupils. Free samples, tokens, raffle tickets, sponsorship, competitions of all sorts, entry forms and coupons constituted for me an occupational hazard that at times I found hard to stomach.

The visiting reverend brother seeking postulants for his order was a yearly caller. Without exception these were gentlemen, but some of the more zealous adopted a modus operandi I found hard to accept. "Will the children who would like to join our order please come out into the corridor one by one"—this after the brother had addressed the senior boys. Rather reluctantly we released the volunteers; invariably some of the happiest rascals in the school decided to relieve the tedium of the school day by volunteering to go out and have a chat with the august visitor. On returning to class some of these lads wore a broad smirk; one or two others who followed were withdrawn and silent. On gently questioning one thoughtful boy about the cause of his apparent concern I was answered bluntly, "He said not to tell you, sir. Nor to tell my father and mother." I thought this the wrong attitude for our visitor to take, and had to use considerable diplomacy to set matters to rights.

My most lively memory concerns a chimney sweep who was recognisable at once as a character. His nickname was Insects.

He was a fine "brave" widower, as black as the hobs of Hell, with a soot-soiled peaked cap jauntily balanced on the side of his head. In early November he enlivened his breast with a row of tarnished medals, souvenirs of the First World War. (A rival said he borrowed them from a pawnshop.) Sporting a waxed moustache and a Kaiser beard, he made a superb entrance into the classroom with his cluster of brushes balanced on his shoulder.

The women teachers intuitively knew that in the matter of love affairs the chimney sweep was still pretty sparky. Turn and turn about the teachers played tricks on one another, and on me if I wasn't on my guard. A young unmarried male teacher recently appointed to the staff constituted for them a slur on the womanhood of Ireland. They considered it their bounden duty to get him married as soon as possible.

One day as both schools poured out into the playground for the eleven o'clock interval, one of the teachers—a widow—remained behind to finish some little chore in her classroom. The sweep arrived at this moment. Another woman teacher, full of divilment, after welcoming the newcomer whispered to him that the woman still in what we called the gallery was on the look-out for a suitable partner. The others confirmed this; they added that it was an opportune time for him to slip in and press his suit. "She'll be shy at first, but you'll be able to handle her," the leader of the conspirators said.

The sweep needed little prompting. Having verified that all the children had been released, he entered the classroom, gently closing the door behind him. One of the female staff adroitly slipped into the school and secured the hasp on the outside of the door, so that neither of the two inside could leave. After a while shrieks of outrage were heard coming from behind the closed door; when, in all innocence, I came along to undo the hasp and investigate the cause of the hubbub, I had to rescue the sweep, for the teacher was belabouring him across the shoulders with her bamboo, no doubt outraged at a rather unconventional and sooty approach to a delicate subject. However, the good woman took it in excellent part and later laughed heartily when the incident was recalled.

From time to time the Society for the Prevention of Cruelty to Animals sent representatives to lecture in the schools. On the occasion of such visits we teachers had great difficulty controlling the exuberance of the children. For some reason they took this visit as one of the great events of the year. We've come a long way since then; I'm sorry to say that fifty years ago awareness of cruelty on this level simply did not exist.

Three cultured women of the old ascendancy entered the largest classroom and gracefully sat down. A young man, a gentle scion of the same stock, delivered a lecture. I have no difficulty in associating myself with the sentiments of this noble organisation; but this lecture seemed to be based on the assumption that the boys were extremely naïve.

If the boys had knowledge of animal cruelty in the area, examples poured out in a flood. They invented lurid details, giving the offenders' names. We teachers grew apprehensive lest, rightly or wrongly, we be blamed for bringing such matters to public notice.

"My mother spikes the hin's nose with timber, sir."

"Why does she do that?"

"To take the hatch out of the hin."

"You promise me you will try to put a stop to that practice?"

"Of course I will, sir."

"My father bit off the pup's tail."

"Why did he do that?"

"To crop it, sir."

"My grandma has a nail on her stick."

"What for?"

"To prod th'ass."

"My granda smothers pusheens."

"Pusheens?"

"Kittens, sir."

And so it went on, much of it invented on the spur of the moment.

The parish priest, who was also the school manager, sometimes referred certain duties to me. When he got letters from America relating to the tracing of relatives I was consulted. One in particular has remained in my mind for sixty years.

Very Reverend and Dear Pastor,

We are an elderly pair, a brother and sister, who live in the southern states of America. Judged even by American standards we are well off. We have no relatives that we know of.

Would you be so kind as to select a boy from an area within a radius of three miles of the local convent school in your town, which our mother attended as a barefooted girl. He should have the same surname as our dear mother when she left your parish in the long ago. So much the better if the child's road to town leads roughly from north to south.

We will of course pay all expenses if you arrange to send him to us in the United States. We also undertake to have him educated in the finest academy in our country. If he proves satisfactory we shall joyfully leave him all our considerable property; if he does not we will send him back to Ireland a well-off man with our blessing. Our bona fides may be checked at the chancery of this diocese.

After checking the bona fides, I approached a cottier with a large family of the correct surname and in the area indicated, and spoke to his wife and himself on the matter. Later I returned to discuss the matter several times. At last a boy was selected, and the family appeared to give the proposal their full agreement. Letters shuttled back and forth to America; eventually, with the apparent good will of all and the imprimatur of the PP, the day drew near for the ticket to be purchased and the little lad to be labelled before being despatched by ship to the United States. As far as I can recall, a nurse was provisionally selected to accompany him on the voyage.

I made a final visit to the cottage to make sure there would be no slip-up in my arrangements. There I was greeted by the gathered family, all crying bitterly. They were inconsolable, so all the plans came to naught.

Somewhat the same thing happened when I was asked by the US embassy to nominate a personable young woman with a certain surname to christen a battleship that was to be named after a commodore of that name who was born in north Kerry. Again, at the last moment the girl's father stepped in and put a stop to her departure. He said that such an expedition would give her notions beyond her years.

Americans called in often, mostly on weekends—second or third-generation Irish returned perhaps to retrace the steps of a grandfather. The fact that sometimes as a boy I had known the grandfather in question was a source of wonder to my visitors. To each of these men his grandfather was someone vague and ethereal, whose boyhood in Ireland was spent wandering in a fairy mist.

There were frequent misunderstandings if the spelling of the surname had suffered a sea change. I grew weary of explaining to these visitors, some of whom were highly educated, that there was no difference between *Mac* and *Mc*. The slightest change of the spelling of the surname and they jibbed at my explanation. No use telling them that my own mother's name was Caughlin, that her many brothers and sisters went to America and Australia and in time their grandchildren returned with spellings of the name ranging from Caughlin to Coghlan, Coughlan, and Cohalan.

One young man refused to accept my assurance that the name pointed out on an old school roll was that of his grandfather. "He spelt it quite differently," he said stoutly. "Do you play the fiddle?" I asked. "How do you know that?" he asked. "Your grandfather and his family were among the most famous fiddlers in this area." Admitting that he was one of the violinists in the New York Philharmonic Orchestra, he then accepted my explanation.

If I did not teach girls, I had many older sisters and young mothers coming to the school door; thus I heard a great deal of confessional material, which must be suppressed. Over the years through these confessions I learnt to appreciate the strengths and weaknesses of an Irish country town.

One incident remains with me after the passage of over fifty years. It concerns a brilliant pupil who for some reason had grown inexplicably "stupid" in class. This condition lasted for several months. His lapse vaguely troubled me, until a neighbouring woman provided the very human explanation—and this without any enquiry on my part. "The boy's mother is going through the menopause. She's very disturbed," she said. "Your pupil sleeps on the bedroom floor holding his mother's hand through the night."

I clearly recall a deputation of holy women calling to the school to interview me. The spokeswoman told me in awesome tones that they had come to ask me to stop the boys from watching the stallions.

Feigning ignorance, "What stallions?" I asked. "The stallions that stand in the stables behind the pub every Friday." "Stallions? Pubs?" from disingenuous me. "They're there to serve the mares. The boys watch them, and it's not good for their immortal souls." I forget exactly how I coped with this. I did nothing, of course. As a boy I had learnt a great deal from those same stables. I thought it more wholesome than much of what passes for sex education today.

Intrusions like this provided me with an idea I later incorporated in a story called "Chestnut and Jet," which describes the pride of a farmer's wife watching her husband leading a stallion through the fair. Perhaps at times the writer in me was more diligent than the teacher.

In my long span both as assistant principal and principal teacher in a typical country town I rarely encountered pederasts in the vicinity of the school. One or two did hang about but they were easily shooed away. Whatever sex there was came naturally to boys in touch with animal life; whatever adventures were those of the wood, the field, and the river.

But I mustn't waste time gossiping. Back to my classroom now, or people will think I didn't teach at all. I seem to sense that publican's fingers slipping along his watch-chain.

CHAPTER SIX

Let me now call attention to a red-letter day in the calendar of the primary school year: the day of enrolment, in which all three components—parents, pupil, and pedagogue—are involved.

All over Ireland, on the first of June or sometimes on one of the later days of May, this enrolment ceremony takes place. It's a day of covenant and commitment. It's a day that calls for rare sensitivity and diplomacy on the part of the teacher, particularly the infant teacher. The covenant implied is seldom if ever overtly expressed: it is nonetheless binding, even legally. If this covenant were to be spoken or written, say by the mother, it would be expressed somewhat as follows:

Dear teacher, because of the demands of our working life, which must be met if we are to provide for our children, his father and I lack the time, energy, technique or knowledge needed to educate this child. We therefore deliver him into your care, trust and control to be trained and educated. You are hereby empowered to exercise over him the same responsibility as would a prudent parent—no more, no less.

It is a day of contagious bawling and mewling. It is also a day of courage and sadness on the part of the parent—usually the mother—who accompanies the child to school. She has cause to feel bereft, yet she tries to remain outwardly calm. For her this is a second weaning: for the first formal time it indicates the child's leaving the home and the comfort of the mother's presence. These securities are traded for an alone-standing among strangers in a new, noisy world. For the mother this day marks the beginning of her child's life of self-reliance, which she must urge upon him if she is worthy of being called mother.

For the child it is a day full of the adventure of growing up. He is now entering the mysterious mansion whence older children have brought back exciting stories. Thus, for him, this special day of initiation is a mixture of elation—and foreboding.

With fistfuls of sweets the gentle trap is baited. Spiderlike, we teachers coax the infants into the web of education.

I pause to note a face among the newcomers. I have taught the little lad's father, having sat in school beside the grandfather. On the features of another boy I see a likeness of his father's or mother's people. "Who's he like?" is a question every new entrant has to endure.

It grows more interesting as the years pass by. A boy who at infant stage seems to resemble none of his parents suddenly turns his profile to the light and there in his glowing, growing features is his mother, picked and painted, as the saying goes. Again it could be a throwaway gesture on the part of the developing lad, and one is tempted to say, "There's old Jamesie born again!" Obviously I could not indulge these reflections in any other than a largely traditional community.

It falls to me as principal to address the assembled mothers. "We teachers will do our best for each child," I say. "If misunderstandings or minor accidents occur, as often happens where there are energetic boys, or if a problem arises to cause you uneasiness, don't keep it to yourself. Please approach the child's teacher or myself and we will do our best to put matters to rights. That's what we're here for. There is no compliment involved. Parents are important to us teachers, but please bear in mind that the school is a society with its own set of rules. In our experience problems tend to disappear once the initial turmoil and upset has died down."

At last, the particulars taken and entered in roll and register, the infants leave the assembly hall and straggle in pairs down the long corridors. They are holding hands, though as yet they are largely unknown to each other. As the days, months and years pass they will come to know each other fully. "My schoolmates," each lad will say; "we sat beside each other on our first day in school."

Where a child sits can be of importance. "Who're you near?" is a question often asked of the child when he returns home. There are often social or family resonances to such a query. The teacher deftly discovers who knows whom. Some parents make whispered suggestions. "Put him near Jimmy: they play together." "From the known to the unknown" is an axiom of teaching.

At last all the children are seated in their classroom; they look up expectantly. They seem to be saying, "Whatever it is we came here for, give it to us and let us go home." The infant teacher, generally but not exclusively a woman, moves quickly about, reassuring a boy who shows unease. Some of the mothers cluster about the classroom doorway. They pretend to chat on other topics but their eyes keep roving to see how their children are bearing up under the ordeal.

The moment of truth is here: for the first time the harness is on the back of the little colt. It is a moment to which teachers are finely attuned. Tears flow among the benches or around the little tables. Tears flow outside too as the mothers try to conceal their pain. Some brave spirits among the children glance coolly around as if to say, "Stop it! Grow up!" These children are too proud to blubber. A snuffle is distinctly heard. It proves to be contagious. One lad weakens completely. "Mommaw," be bleats. Others follow suit. Outside the doorway the mother of the lamb grows red with mortification. The teacher reassures the parent. "He'll be fine when you leave. He cries only because he knows you're here." The mother pauses. How can she resist the urge to enter the room and console the wailer?

When the teacher gives him an attractive toy he blubbers to a stop. One by one the mothers drag themselves away from the doorway. Later in the morning one or two will return, saying, "I was just passing and I thought I'd look in to see how Paudie was doing. May I see him for a minute?" Paudie sobs his way through the reunion; later the sorrow of parting begins anew. It is a lovely natural process, which experienced infant teachers are used to dealing with.

After a time—seldom a tranquil period—most of the children settle down. Not all do, however: some carry non-cooperation and even revolt to unusual lengths, at times keeping it up for weeks. They have been known to break loose, to claw the teacher and to kick her shin. Each of these little rebels has to be treated individually.

We found it hard to know what one brave lad was wailing about. He would keep up his courage for an hour or two, then for no reason that his teacher and I could identify he would begin to cry inconsolably. We both put our ears close to his face and heard the word "Thomas" recurrent in his lament. When the caoin slowed to full audibility we solved the problem. He was repeating over and over, "Lift me up and gimme wan look at Thomas. Then I'll be fine." We realised that his older brother was in the classroom just outside the glass partition of the infants' room. So we lifted the infant and, tapping the glass, called the teacher's attention to the fact that we wished the older brother to be allowed leave his place and approach the pane through which we were peeping. Thomas did so and gestured lovingly. The infant then knuckled his eyes dry and smiled bravely. "I'm fine now," he said. "Ye can put me down."

This ritual had to be repeated every hour or so, the interval gradually extending until one look per day was enough to charge the child's batteries. This ration of brotherly love was unnecessary after a week or so. "Wan look at Thomas" was a byword in the staff room for some time.

Not all infants are as gentle as this. The school had been presented with a half-lifesize wooden horse, which was kept in the infant department, then temporarily housed in an upper room of the library across the road while school repairs were in progress.

It was my custom to reward a newly enrolled infant by placing him on the back of this horse and rocking him back and forth. "I hope you enjoyed your ride on the horse," I said to one little novice outside the school gate. The child scowled up at me and said, "Yourself and your bloody horse, ye frightened the life outa me!"

And if that wasn't retort enough I found that some of these same infants referred to me as "Master MacMahon with the high legs"—because the infant teachers wore skirts and I wore long trousers.

Children reared by their grandparents or other older people, especially if they lived in the rural part of the school area, were always a source of delight. An adult layer of thought and word superimposed on the infant mind resulted in a delightful precociousness of attitude and expression in a dialect used to effect by local playwrights, including myself.

One such lad recently enrolled trotted by my side for a hundred yards or so to his point of pick-up for being taken home. It was a bitter winter afternoon of intermittent squalls of hail. Suddenly he looked up at me and in the exact piping voice of his grandmother said, "I'm tellin' you, master, 'twill make a night for the fire."

I was very fortunate that the infant teachers encouraged the emergence of a personality among the infants. Believe it or not, we rejoiced at finding such a jewel, especially a young extrovert. We were farsighted enough to appreciate that encouragement at the chrysalis stage would serve him all his life.

It was important to realise that the country children could understand the point of a joke that was Greek to children with an urban background. "I wonder now would she folly a bucket?" This comment, which had reference, God save us, to the difficulty of bringing the body of a fat woman out of a small room, is completely lost on town children, who have no idea what the others are laughing at. "Don't tell them!" I shouted at the country children from my place in class. If the urban reader reminds himself of a farm animal in a paddock, he may see the point of the joke.

Nothing causes more consternation or anguish in a school than the lost child. No matter how close the surveillance, some child will leave the school environs.

One of our missing children I particularly recall. After about an hour and a half of searching I found him at last in a niche at the back of the play-shed, nestling among a pile of builders' boards. He was crouched there frozen and badly soiled. The memory of the moment when the shivering boy looked up at me, his eyes desolated with the treachery of his bowels, which had robbed him of his dignity, remains with me to this day.

In the little kitchen of the school I plugged in the electric kettle. A bigger boy, needless to say not from an affluent family, took charge of mishaps like this. He was a born comforter; the staff had marked him as becoming a nurse—even a doctor if home circumstances were otherwise. He was in charge of the bag of sawdust and the small shovel. "You'll be all right, boy," he said as he began to cleanse the little fellow, and later gave him a cup of tea.

In time this bigger lad left school and emigrated to England. Many years later, when I had forgotten him almost completely, I saw a tall, immaculately dressed young man being joyfully hailed by a crowd of children returning from school. I suddenly realised who it was as the children shouted his name. He thrust his hand deep in his pockets, took out a fist of silver and threw it up in the air for the children to squabble over. Still smiling, he strutted away. Obviously during his years abroad in some walk of life his sense of caring had brought him reward.

The infants continue to be interesting in their uniqueness. Again I record my appreciation of the dedicated infant teacher who sees her role as an extension of motherhood and who solves problems by intuition. I had to solve difficulties by other means. The average infant is distrustful of a large, able-bodied man such as I was. Every day as the hundred or more infants passed me by on the corridor I covertly watched their eyes for even the slightest flicker of fear. This I had to banish by some means or other, else it would persist and later cause me misunderstanding. The solution came to me by accident.

As they moved past me I pretended to be engrossed in thought. One of the infants whom I knew personally, as I was frequently a visitor in his parents' home, pulled me by the jacket to attract my attention. I pretended to be alarmed; the children knew that my fright was faked; so the practice of pulling the teacher's jacket spread until it became a laughing game. Later an infant was valorous enough to pull my hand. Again the others followed suit.

For me this was more than a game. When the last wavering mite had dared to pull my sleeve, my coat-tails, or my hand, somehow I sensed that all were released from the bondage of fear.

Such children do have genuine fears. Their eyes give them away. One is frightened by the presence of a boy bigger than himself; another hides behind a bigger boy when someone smaller than himself approaches. Another is terrified by an overhanging projection. Among them are nail-biters, eye-scratchers, clawers, jersey-draggers, eaters of mortar and putty, runaways, and incipient fiction writers who already have begun to tell embroidered lies.

I do not think that it is part of the teacher's duty to convey to the children the false notion that life is devoid of malice, injury, ill fortune, treachery, or injustice. Rather should he somehow convey the manner in which these traitors should be downfaced, dodged, or overcome. But somehow or other he should never cease to promote in children the determination to say "Yes" to life, to the dark as well as to the bright of it, to its beauty and glory, to its lapses from grace into degradation and its eventual restoration to serenity. Thus it is that as a person, the teacher needs to be carefully selected, not for false piety or similar inferior motive but above all for an infectious enthusiasm allied to knowledge in its widest sense.

There has been in the past a reluctance by parents to send a mildly retarded child to school. Public attitudes have altered dramatically: such children nowadays live in boarding schools, and there are day clinics and centres of training or care in which children with special needs have the opportunity to realise their potential. The reluctance has all but vanished, and good riddance to it.

Any teacher of my vintage will tell of the beneficial influence on a class of the presence of a disadvantaged child. It was as if he created an aura that evoked a protective atmosphere of affection from the other children. I often talk of the "gifts" each child possesses and that the teacher must seek to evoke. I am then asked, "What gift has such a boy?" and I answer, "Perhaps he has the greatest gift of all: the gift of love." This can be glibly said, of course, but it happens to be true.

Such boys were fully accepted in my day, were loved and loving, and were protected by their classmates. If even a casual slight were directed at the disadvantaged lad from any quarter I watched out for the sudden flare of anger in the eyes of his classmates, some of whom were considered to be the roughest lads in school.

This reflex helped me to see each would-be protector in a better light, and often caused me to revise my attitude towards him in class. The disadvantaged lad was encouraged to take part in the outdoor activities; in the case of a football match he was given a post of responsibility off the field. It was a cause of satisfaction to me in later years that such a boy took his place in the local community, according to his ability, but nonetheless honoured for that. When one of these lads, now grown to a young adult, was knocked down by a car and almost killed, the whole town grieved. The number of townspeople who came to visit him in the hospital was so great that, in ones and twos, the hospital staff made their way to his bedside to see what manner of patient had drawn such a host of wellwishers.

I am reminded of the words spoken by the father of such a young man. "They are all gone now," he said, referring to his seven other children, who had left home and prospered in many fields. "I'm left with Johnny, who gives me back more love than all the others put together."

This attitude of understanding applied also to the epileptic child in school. As is well known, such children get and give a warning of an oncoming fit in a highly individual way. I had stationed two sensible boys on either side of a pupil thus stricken, to provide immediate protection if the fit came on. At times in mid-class the warning whine went up from the little patient, to be followed by a heart-rending moan and a series of troubled spasms and gesticulations. The "minders" adapted naturally to this recurrent crisis and were able to cope before I could approach. If one of the pair happened to be answering a question at the time, he would rarely break the course of his reply while continuing to attend the patient.

In the end it got so that boys vied with each other to be given the task of guardian. Some of the would-be nurses even bribed the patient to be allowed to serve in this task of honour. I think the little epileptic lad knew very little of what was happening at the time of crisis, but his ego was boosted by the attention and deference he always received.

Special needs, individual attention—some children demand it if they are to survive. Large classes are a stain on any education system. The child with stammering or poor articulation is a source of serious concern to his parents. A sense of shame, born of the fear of the child being ridiculed in public, often caused the parents to postpone his entry into school. Without stressing the matter I did my best to present a calm attitude when at last the child was led to the school door. "Everything will come all right," I'd say. And so it does if there is no physical auditory problem.

I once attended a university staff party in the United States where the guest of honour was a doctor considered one of the world authorities on stammering in children. Hearing that I was an Irish teacher he accosted me bluntly and asked, "Hey, teacher, what do you do about kids who stammer?"

I wasn't prepared for such a confrontation, and murmured the usual things about breathing and humming. I mentioned that in a school play a boy who suffered badly lost his stammer on temporarily changing his identity. Somehow as I talked, I felt I was making a fool of myself.

The specialist growled a rejection of my efforts to explain. "But what do you really do in class with a kid like that?" he insisted. I fell back on what I really did. "On the first day, at the first titter of laughter I stare the other boys into silence. I then call the sufferer to the front of the class and quietly address the other children. 'Each of you has been sent to the turf shed for an armful of turf for the fire. Perhaps you have taken too many sods and some have fallen to the ground. So it is with Patrick here. Overeager to please us by his answer, he lets words fall and can't pick them up. We all understand for Patrick, so we'll help him out, won't we?' The class respond with a gentle murmur." "That's about as far as *I've* got in a lifetime of study," the specialist growled as he walked away.

Just as surely as each artist betrays himself in some recurrent mannerism, in brushwork or in written word, so also under the pressure of asking or answering a question in class, each child does so to the accompaniment of an idiosyncratic gesture or ritual. One boy reduces his eyes to slits, another half-closes his fist and shakes it, another scratches his breast, another pushes his little finger up his nostril, another worries his ear, another shuffles his shoe. It is a highly individual mannerism, even though at times the signal is so faint that it cannot be readily apprehended. This distinctive gesture persists until the boy becomes an adult.

One of the most poignant experiences for a teacher in a primary school is to see a pale, drawn face at the glass panel of a classroom door and to know at once that something has happened. A neighbouring girl, a sister of one of the pupils, is outside. "Can I have Mícheál home?" she asks me in a low voice. "Something wrong, Mary?" "His father has just dropped dead," she says in broken tones. "Oh, oh, oh," I murmur in sympathy, and then turn to the gently buzzing room. It falls silent as I enter. I speak to the class for a moment or two on some other subject, as if the girl's arrival were not of the supreme importance it is and also to allay sudden alarm. As gently as I dare I then say, "Mícheál, you're wanting at home, son. Mary is outside the door to take you down. Yes, take your schoolbag." The boy turns his head, reads Mary's face, and his features drain of all colour. As I lead him to the door a meaningful silence falls behind me. The boy knows that his world will never be the same again.

For me the saddest experience of all was to see the body of a drowned boy. He had been transferred a short time before from my school to the school adjoining, and as the pupils poured out onto the roadway in the afternoon he raced to the river to have a swim after a broiling day in class. When the alarm was raised, with others I rushed to the riverside. It was heartbreaking to see him stretched out on the summer grass, his purple togs still on his buttocks, looking so tranquil that he could have been asleep. But attempts at resuscitation had failed, and the child was as dead as could be.

I saw these infants climb the ladder of the years. To this day I covertly watch their progress. In common with many teachers, I have a proprietary interest in them. In the secret recesses of my mind they have names other than those given them by their parents. There's My Daddy, Wristwatch, Kerryman, Question Mark, Boarding School, Shouter, Shilling, Chalkie, Plasticine, One-Look, No-Pinch, Sawdust, Dracula, T'ilet, and Bellman.

Dracula, from his earliest years, was obsessed with films about Count Dracula, while T'ilet was instructed at home to shout "Toilet" if he wished to leave the classroom. Bellman, when last I saw him, was a business executive studying the pages of the *New York Times*. I never, never use these names in public—they are for private filing only.

My most precious image is of Daffodil. I see the doorknob in my classroom turning and a Down's Syndrome boy entering, the broadest of smiles on his face and a single daffodil in his hand.

CHAPTER SEVEN

The scene was a garden party attended by dignitaries of the Church of England. It was held in an interval of the Lambeth or some similar conference. Relaxing from debate, the bishops basked in gracious surroundings, drinking tea and eating cake. An Irish maid waiting on the guests approached the table at which her employer, the host bishop, was seated. She held out a plate of confectionery.

"No, Bridget," the bishop said, "I won't indulge. At my age, indulgence is not recommended."

"Does the maid know what indulgence means?" another bishop asked impishly.

The host bishop looked up. "What is indulgence, Bridget?" he asked.

Without a pause the maid answered, "Indulgence is a remission of the whole or part of the temporal punishment due to the divine justice for sin, after sin and the eternal punishment have been remitted."

Her employer sipped his tea and, looking over the rim of his cup at his brother bishops, said, with a twinkle in his eye, "Perhaps, after all, that is how Christian doctrine should be taught."

We primary teachers of the years following the establishment of the state carried two heavy burdens in the line of duty, this although we were badly housed and badly paid.

It was enjoined upon us by the state to undertake the revival of Irish as a spoken language, a task that, by and large, we manfully faced; and it was also enjoined upon us by the Catholic Church, which, to put it at its mildest, was powerful at that time, to transfer from one generation to the next the corpus of Catholic belief, then as now the faith of the overwhelming majority of the pupils in Irish schools.

Officially the schools were considered non-sectarian. There was a notice printed on cardboard and hung on the wall of every classroom. One side bore the legend *Religious Instruction*, the other side, *Secular Instruction*. When Christian doctrine was being taught, the card had to be turned outwards to indicate this, and vice versa—otherwise the teacher could be reprimanded; although, to be honest, this practice was more often ignored than followed.

Early in my teaching career I found myself at Christmastime in Cashel of the Kings in Co Tipperary. There, one frosty morning, I joined a bunch of local lads who, followed by a motley pack of terriers and a half-greyhound, were off for a day's hunting in the fields north of the famous Rock. The huntsmen made straight for a spacious field in the centre of which a walled enclosure contained a little burial ground. "We'll find Butler here," one of my comrades said cryptically.

"Butler?" I asked Mick the Huntsman as we turned homeward. "Why the name?"

"Did you never hear of the Most Reverend James Butler, who published the famous penny catechism recommended by the four Catholic archbishops of Ireland as a general catechism for the kingdom?" he replied. "The hare we call Butler has a form on his grave."

"*That* Dr Butler!" I knew all about him; I had cause to do so. So that was where he was buried. Immediately I thought of Bridget at the garden party. More than most people, I knew where she had learnt her definition of indulgence.

Butler's catechism, by order of the bishop, was in use in the diocese of Kerry during the greater part of my life as a teacher. It was a little book printed on cheap paper, its pages held together by a single staple, and could be slipped easily into a pocket. It contained 112 pages in all, some 86 in question-and-answer form. There were no illustrations.

Much of the knowledge we imparted in the Christian doctrine lesson was abstract. One of the things we had to explain to children who were scarcely ten years old was that when a person died and went to Heaven his body joined his soul on the last day and was then endowed with attributes that it did not possess while on earth: agility, subtility, and brightness. I carefully explained the meaning of each of these words. Agility meant that the body now had the power to move faster than lightning from place to place, no matter how far apart these places were, either on earth or in space; subtility signified that the body could then pass through material objects without hindrance; brightness meant that wherever it went the now glorified body took with it the shining glory of Heaven.

By the end of his primary school period every pupil was presumed to have learnt by rote almost all the contents of this little book, with its total of perhaps 25,000 words. This included one answer—running to a total of 170 words—that purported to offer with absolute accuracy proof of the existence of Purgatory.

This stout information provided the child, possibly destined for the emigrant boat, with an answer calculated to confound humanists, atheists, agnostics, or even HG Wells himself.

I consider the greatest mistake any commentator can make in matters of this kind is to pass judgement on "then" in the context of "now." To do so is to ignore, either through ignorance or deceit, the prevailing atmosphere of a particular era and hold it up to unjust scrutiny or ridicule by applying to it standards that nowadays prevail in a completely altered set of circumstances. Superficial radio and television commentators, even historians of the shallower kind, are dab hands at this shabby practice: quite often by claptrap they evoke a cheap laugh or a spurious burst of applause. Statesmen long dead and institutions like the Catholic Church are the chief targets.

This is not to infer that great institutions cannot learn from the errors of the past. For my part there was never a time in my career when I did not realise that Butler's catechism had long outlived its hour and was doing positive harm. It smacked of medievalism; it reeked with condemnation; it had a negative approach to what was positive and sublime. Were it not for the Second Vatican Council, or the course of thought that led up to that council, Butler's catechism might still persist as the basis of Catholic teaching in the schools of my native Kerry, where the standard demanded was unbelievably high.

For a full month before the visit of the diocesan examiner very little else was done in any class except the revision of the parrot-like responses to the questions in the little book.

Catechism questions, and those arising from the text, covered all aspects of faith. They included what was required and forbidden by each of the Ten Commandments as well as by the Precepts of the Church, the qualities of contrition and of confession, the impediments to matrimony, the Seven Gifts of the Holy Ghost, the matter, form and sensible sign of each sacrament, as well as its scriptural proof, the distinction between fast and abstinence—this the children found most difficult to grasp—and the distinction between *latria*, the supreme worship offered to God, *hyperdulia*, the worship offered to the Virgin Mary, and *dulia*, the reverence paid to saints and angels. Also included were the Scriptural and Corporal Works of Mercy, the Eight Beatitudes, the Divine Praises, the fifteen mysteries of the Rosary, and a host of other matters.

It's now time for me to pause and clarify my motives for writing in this strain. I look upon my church not alone as a vehicle for my faith but also as a fruitful source of my culture. To me, the turning year is meaningless if not viewed through the focused lens of Christianity.

But as regards religious instruction in school, I was forced to deal with the rigidity of faith. My mind resembled a pair of binoculars held the wrong way around, through which for the most part I viewed the projection of my religion as something miniaturised, the details reduced to remoteness, coldness, and abstraction.

There were times outside school when through the liberation of literature I was enabled to turn the binoculars the right way around and see the dimensions of the Christian experience in forms far more spacious. I was often compelled to wonder if the polarities as I experienced them in this instance could ever be reconciled or harmonised.

Again and again I asked myself what effect Butler's catechism and my interpretation of it was having on the minds of schoolchildren. Grown to manhood, how would the children comport themselves in the face of adversity? Was I branding them with a sense of guilt or endowing them with a sense of glory? Where was the source of solace, and where the hope that follows it? To me, an old priest turning slowly to face a congregation and looking over his glasses to say, "We are all sinners," and then turning away again could be more effective than the outpourings of a province of pulpit-thumping Redemptorists—for such they then were. Solace? In terms that were pagan I found this in the pages of James Stephens's *Crock of Gold,* in which the polarities of human nature are at least set out before the reader.

> *Man is a god and a brute. He aspires to the stars with his head but his feet are contented in the grasses of the field, and when he forsakes the brute upon which he stands, then there will be no more men and no more women and the immortal gods will blow this world away like smoke.*

Where does this leave me? Some smidgin of this outlook, as I see it, is included in the better manifestations or aspirations of the Second Vatican Council. Reconciliation is the password that opened the gate of understanding. And about time too.

Nevertheless, in these latter days phrases from the old catechism—"Exclusion from the house of God whilst living and deprived of Christian burial when they die...Out of Hell there is no redemption...Incur much more the wrath of God"—continue to haunt my memory.

During my time as a teacher I left theology to those better equipped to expound it, but I continued to see my own particular and possibly idiosyncratic belief as a cultural treasure-house. This may suggest a demeaning of the spiritual dimension. I hope not: I simply set down the attitude that was truly mine.

I had pity for the diocesan examiner doing his rounds of the schools, for this must have been truly soul-destroying work unless the man had the spiritual reserves of a pilgrim saint. As a result of this inspection the school was marked in a manner similar to that which obtained in secular subjects: "very satisfactory," "satisfactory," or "unsatisfactory." If in the published report of the schools of the diocese the significant contraction *Uns.* appeared after the name of a school, that institution was in the black books of parish and diocese.

The day of the bishop! Confirmation day is still one of immense importance in the life of an Irish parish; although nowadays the approach to the sacrament is far more benign, and as a consequence the grace of the occasion shines through. I recall the former fear of the event, leavened as it was by ice-cream, box cameras, and pockets of pence. The ice-cream still holds its own, though in a more varied and finger-lickin' form, while the copper coins have been replaced with fivers and tenners, and the box camera has yielded place to the Camcorder.

Sunlight streaming through stained-glass windows throws scarves of colour on the ranked boys and girls. Presently the bishop moves out of the sanctuary to begin his examination of the children. That examination in the olden days! In front of the parishioners! The teacher was hard set to win in this religious arena. If a child failed it was the teacher's fault; a sidelong word or query to one of the clergy and the bishop (had he been told in advance by the diocesan examiner where the weakness lay?) made straight for the weakest link in the chain. Now and again as the bishop examined a pupil his eyes rolled sidelong to see if the teacher was prompting a slow answerer. The teacher trembled lest the bishop ask a child to hand up his ticket; in even more stringent days the ticket could be dramatically torn up to indicate rejection, and the child—even though he was a travelling child a bare week in school and put forward for the sacrament by a sentimental curate—put back for Confirmation on another date in another parish. This was the ultimate shame.

This is perhaps the time to recall a degradation of Confirmation time that was on its way out when I began to teach. I refer to the "servants' class." This was composed of boys—rarely girls—who had left the school after third or fourth class to go into service with farmers or shopkeepers. Before the School Attendance Act of 1926 these young men and women, many from families who had lost fathers in the First World War, became poor school attenders. After First Communion they tended to drift away but would later be rounded up for Confirmation.

I can see them clearly now as they presented themselves at school for a few weeks before the bishop's arrival, there to be crammed like pre-Christmas geese with the elements of Christian doctrine.

They shambled rather than walked; an odd one secretly sucked a broken clay pipe; others, I feared, slept in outhouses. They were branded as cannon fodder in imperial wars. Their great-grandfathers had seen the "sepoys" chained to cannon wheels in India and then blown to pieces; their grandfathers had fought in the Boer War; their fathers had heeded the recruiting sergeant who urged the labourers' sons to answer Kitchener's call, "Your king and country need you."

On a quiet Saturday morning, whenever I turned up the old school registers, inevitably I found the chill entry *Gone in service* after the names of many boys who left school after the third or fourth class in the 1920s. Thankfully, by the late 1930s such entries no longer appear.

There was one reprehensible incident in a place I will not identify. The parish priest always took it as a personal affront if one of the schools under his control failed to acquit itself adequately on Confirmation day. On the failure of one or two children to reply properly, the bishop needed only to glance at the local priest as if to say, "Is this how you fulfil your parochial duties? Do I have to mention your record in Rome on my next visit?" for the faces of the clergy to appear crestfallen.

On one such occasion the PP spoke from the pulpit on the Sunday following Confirmation. In solemn tones he declared, "Most of the schools in my parish answered well, except for the school taught by Mrs —. What wonder is that? She's hardly fit to feed pigs, not to mention teach the word of God."

Uproar followed. The woman in question complained, either directly or perhaps through her organisation, to the bishop, who in turn ordered the priest to retract publicly what he had said. The following Sunday the priest again addressed the people. "Regarding what I said last Sunday about a certain lady teacher when I stated she was not fit to feed pigs: I retract that statement completely. In my opinion she has a great warrant to do so." The hullabaloo that followed this odd recantation can well be imagined. Suffice it to say that the bishop's order finally prevailed.

Nowadays the main problem is not a proof of the existence of Purgatory or Limbo but how to face the commonplace denial of the existence of a supreme being. Children are now moving into a society where God is mocked: try mentioning his name in the average secular university in the United States and brace yourself for the explosion that follows.

Naïve as I am, it has always appeared to me that every religious text in use in every school class should obliquely—and poetically,

The Master aged twenty

The Master in his classroom in the old school
(photo: *Holiday*, USA)

The first Listowel Writers' Week workshop; 1973

Lighting the Christmas candle
(The candle was made by Smiths of Killarney and burned for the whole twelve days of Christmas)
(photo: Kevin Coleman, the *Kerryman*)

Bryan and his late wife, Kitty, on the day in 1991 when Kitty, a
lover of flowers, learned that a camellia named
"Kitty MacMahon of Listowel" had won a major award in the US
(photo: Brendan Landy, Listowel)

Bronze head by Marjorie F Fitzgibbon ARHA

Three Kerry storytellers (Bryan MacMahon, John B Keane and Eamon Kelly)
(photo: Brendan Landy)

The Master today
(photo: Brendan Landy)

if at all possible—stress or convey, even by implication, the knowledge of God as shown in his creation: the painted trout in the stream; the computer in the head of the elver enabling the little wriggler to find its way over thousands of miles of ocean floor and reach its destination in the headwaters of an Irish stream; the miracle of the mushroom; the husbandry of the ant colony.

The camera of the human eye; the everyday phenomena of conception and parturition, the cunning and delectable fashion in which man and woman mortise and tenon to form new human beings; the swing of the seasons; the layers of rock upreared into mountains—the mind falters and surrenders on the contemplation of space and its innumerable planets, each allotted its duty and station. Did all these emerge from Nothing to be cherished and governed by No-One?

Calling attention to the proofs of the existence of a supreme being from the evidence of nature without due reference to revelation and the teaching of Jesus Christ is, I am aware, fraught with danger from the viewpoint of the Catholic theologian. The result, he fears, will be the emergence of a new or old type of humanist, one who urges abstention from theorising and who may acknowledge a god of nature as distinct from the god of the Testaments. But this is a risk that surely must be taken.

My mother, God rest her, had a store of wise sayings, some of which have remained with me when the minutiae of scriptural exegesis have been forgotten. "The Ten Commandments are as good for your body as they are for your soul." I haven't always heeded her advice, but I have done tolerably well when one takes the human dimension into the reckoning.

I have wandered from the rooms of my noisy mansion. Looking back, I do not know how we who then taught survived, or even how the faith we were ordered to transfer remained intact when one considers the exigencies of fear under which we worked. The daily half-hour class was gobbled up by the individual examination of the forty to fifty children answering by rote the questions of the day. Recitations of prayer, explanations and hymns had me wondering if there was any time to teach the real beauty of the word of God.

Today the textbooks on religious knowledge are a joy to see and to handle, and must surely be a delight to teach. I'd like to place on record that in the opening years of the final decade of the present millennium, relations between pastor priest and parishioners are on a high plane of cordiality, appreciation, and understanding.

Leaving a church after a funeral Mass, I fell into step with a man who had spent a lifetime abroad and who had a keen awareness of life on many levels. "I hope," he said, "that the quality of ceremony and the comfort of the priest's homily will never die out in Ireland." The true priest has many roles: he is healer, guide, and comforter. He is also scapegoat, since he often bears the weight of the secret sins of his parish. And because of his training and the nature of his calling, he stands alone.

Which reminds me that small boats should keep close to shore, so I will paddle my curach back to the little harbour I left on the morning tide. As I do so I renew my plea for additional stress to be placed on the cultural and artistic side of our religious belief. The priest and the artist are closer to each other than either knows: for one thing, both vouch for the precious nature of the individual body, imagination, or soul.

Back with me to the classroom. The various feast-days of the year have always had a huge impact on school life. St Brigid's Day saw the weaving of the traditional rush crosses in class; St

Patrick's Day with its harp and shamrock and its parade is a delight for children. Eastertide—a German boy brought decorated eggs, which we kept on display for a number of years. And so on through the year to the feast of the Nativity, the beauty of which for the children never palls. And if it does, for me and countless others a good substitute would have to be invented to endow darkest winter with even the tawdriest of meanings.

CHAPTER EIGHT

S o far I have dealt with the schoolroom part of my life. The school bell ringing at three o'clock signalled my entry into the other part. What was that part doing all the time? Preparing? At rest and at peace? Restless?

Multifarious and hyperactive—these are the adjectives that come to mind. Balance between the two component parts of my mind and body was possible, but only after the gentle barrier of sleep was interposed. Otherwise I could not have lasted longer than a month. All the time I was vitally interested in what another might term the trivialities of a small town. I had five sons, each a person in his own right, and a good wife, who guaranteed domestic harmony and bliss.

During the war years I had kept my bookshop open; the experience made me realise that if I were sacked by sensitive authorities, lay or clerical, for something I had written, I could earn a better living than teaching by getting my hands on a yard of shop counter. By this time I had discovered that one cannot overcome the troubles of the mind except by dodging them. Occupational therapy it's called nowadays.

I played handball and hurling; beagled on Sundays; continued to be enthralled by folklore, dialect, and racial memory; mastered Irish; subscribed to literary magazines from England and America; trained myself to listen to the most outwardly unprepossessing persons.

I attended traditional gatherings such as Puck Fair, the Ballyvourney Fitchin (Whitsun), and Garland Sunday in Lahinch, and wandered here and there in Ireland. The secret language of the roads took my attention. To me the islands off the west coast were fairylands.

I wrote stories and articles for *The Bell*—praises to Ó Faoláin and O'Connor. Wrote plays—"The novel is a man's lawful wife, but the stage is his flashy mistress." Helped found the local drama group. Produced a play or two, and adjudicated at a drama festival. Took time off to write and print ballads on scores of topics.

Lectured here and there as the humour took me. Continued to be astonished at the reception my first collection of short stories received in America. Continued to walk the quiet streets each night with my old friend Ned Sheehy. Visited by Dick Dodd of Georgia, a man who altered my outlook on life and who remains an old and understanding friend. Was part of almost every local organisation—except those that were political. Subscribed to Dublin postal libraries: Switzer's was good, and the RDS was generous. Had a branch of the Argosy Library in my bookshop, so I had the privilege of selecting my own titles.

The fact that I had set out deliberately to widen the horizons of experience and perception made me appreciate my place in the scheme of my life.

Is there such a person as a typical schoolteacher? Male teachers have been stigmatised as "men among children and children among men."

By way of defence it must be said that one cannot stand in front of a class for a lifetime, relying on all kinds of shifts to capture and retain children's attention, without gaining certain mannerisms in the process.

One of my sons returned from school one day and confessed himself disgusted with the classroom antics of his father; I was illustrating an old woman paddling on the beach in Ballybunion, and had raised my trouser legs in the process.

Most of my fellow-teachers as I knew them were highly intelligent men and women who, as secondary students, found themselves in a buyer's market. Motivated by their parents, they had moved into teaching as a steady means of earning a livelihood. The "call to training" was something prized in the days when university education was not yet open to all who reached the high standard demanded and whose parents had the money to pay fees and "digs." The subsidised training as a teacher and the permanent salary that followed—the "standing thing," as it was called—appealed to the sons and daughters of teachers, small farmers, and minor officials—increasingly so for young women, as a desirable way of "doing for" members of large families.

Some teachers in training were products of cramming schools, others were former clerical students. A few with basic BA degrees were exempt from the first of the two years spent in training. Sixty years ago a large number came from the preparatory schools: the pupils of these schools were recruited at Intermediate level and educated with a teaching career in mind. These preparatory colleges were closed after some years, as a result of a gear-change in official thinking, possibly because of the public comment that moulding would-be teachers as if they were clerical students in a monastic atmosphere was contrary to the broader principles of education.

Whatever road was taken, the government of the day acquired these students cheaply, trained them cheaply, and, hand in glove with the ecclesiastical authorities, sent them out into the land confident that, subject to rigid inspection, they would display the qualities of dedication, humility, and obedience. Which, to a considerable extent, they did.

Did these men and women realise their full potential? Could they have won higher acclaim and reward in other stations in life? This depends on the individual outlook and a host of other circumstances. A few of them defected to radio in its early days and made their mark in that medium. Most took up teaching posts in various parts of the country and earned respect, often under difficult conditions. They taught in remote islands and in city slums. They gave unstinted service to the GAA: the spread of national games in the last century came initially from Erin's Hope, the team representing St Patrick's College. Others gave loyal service to organisations such as Comhaltas Ceoltóirí Éireann and Conradh na Gaeilge. As a group they loved Ireland and the things of Ireland, and were the pillars of the communities in which they taught.

Some immersed themselves in music, archaeology, or folklore. They wrote local guides, and were called on as authorities on local history and genealogy. Some loved learning for its own sake. Lacking comradely stimulus, others took to the bottle, to become eccentrics or alcoholics. Finding themselves in an area where there was an overbearing parish priest who brooked no rivals in parochial status, some became either subservient or rebellious.

Everywhere in Ireland a "character" is loved. This is equally true of the priest and the teacher. Anyone who is a source of anecdotal marvels, quips and adventures for the ordinary people is prized for conversation, and sometimes for the feeling of superiority it occasions in the mind of the narrator. Teachers are no exceptions to this rule, either as subjects or objects of local stories.

When teachers get together and let down their hair they tend to talk about those in their ranks who border on the quirky and wayward. The inevitable anecdote has an extra touch of sauce to it when it describes a joust with an inspector or someone in authority. "What I said to the inspector" was the subject of much of what passed between teachers when they met on social occasions.

The hotel porter occupied a significant place in the annals of small-town and village education. The hackney driver too. They could be relied on to pass the word along when a divisional inspector was in the vicinity. Sheer panic seized the teaching body in the old days when word went out that a "divisional" was in town. I recall the tremor in my mother's voice when she said, "Don't upset me tonight, children, I may have a head inspector in the morning."

Each school had its own early warning system. If an inspector got into the school premises without being observed, the first teacher to spot him despatched a boy with a stick of white chalk to the door of each classroom, telling the boy to say to the teacher, "Here's the white chalk you asked for." A stick of coloured chalk indicated a man straight from the department in Marlborough Street. And when central heating came, the pipes passing from room to room when struck with a ruler—the same technique as used in prisons—gave notice that an outsider had gained entrance.

Many of the school inspectors knew of this practice and tended to connive at it: many of them had risen in the ranks from being teachers themselves. One inspector friend of mine told me that while daydreaming at the wheel of his car he had driven past a little country school and, realising what he had done, had parked his car and retraced his steps on foot. He knew there was generally a boy on sentry duty near a window— the warning cry was, "Car goin' slow, sir!"—so he gave ample time for the warning to be given. On his leisurely entry, the inspector found the schoolmaster standing on a high stool, peering out the tall window of the gable. The moment the inspector set foot in the classroom he heard the teacher saying backwards over his shoulder to the class, "And the bastard never even called, boys!"

However fictitious that tale may be, I can vouch for the truth of the following. An inspector had been despatched to issue a final notice to a Kerry schoolmaster who, when the humour took him, dismissed his scholars and, with his beloved fiddle in hand, took to the open road. The inspector was having breakfast in the hotel when he happened to glance out the dining-room window. Whom should he see but the master himself, fiddling furiously amid the fair-day throng of farmers and beasts. Nothing if not human, the inspector whispered into the porter's ear, "Go out and tell the fiddler to get to his school as fast as he can. If he is there before the inspector arrives, there won't be a word about it." Some time later this master abandoned his school in favour of the life of a wandering fiddler, and his name is enshrined in local balladry.

The echoes of long-dead schoolteachers live after them in unusual ways. When I visit a certain village I prick up my ears and listen to the local conversation to find if the labour of an old schoolmaster has been in vain. This man spent his life battling against the curtailment of the suffix *ing* to *in'*. "Coming, going, buying, selling, teaching, learning," he would chant, with the accent on the ending. It became a passion with him. When I hear "He was com-ing," or "She was fly-ing," I breathe a prayer for the old grammarian.

I heard of an old country schoolmaster who was too fastidious, or too proud, to be seen approaching the latrines in the school yard. When lunchtime came he locked himself in his classroom and urinated into the fireplace. The pupils were puzzled by the fact that a roaring fire was sometimes almost quenched on their return to the classroom.

Sometimes there are minor feuds among the members of the staff, perhaps maintained after the cause of the differences is forgotten. Place a pair of feuding teachers in charge of different classes in one large classroom and a subtle confrontation is inevitable. I heard of one such war of attrition.

In guerrilla fashion it was carried on by a pair of women teachers through the medium of the handwriting or headlines, usually proverbs, on each of the two blackboards at opposite ends of the same classroom. *Put a beggar on horseback and she'll ride to the devil* would be countered by *If you lie down with the dogs you get up with the fleas*. These the innocent pupils dutifully copied in their best handwriting.

I am often asked what are the characteristics of a good teacher. It is presumptive of me to reply, yet I do so for what it is worth.

Dedication is a prime requisite, as is the gift of infectious enthusiasm. A sense of humour that does not wound is desirable, since it tends to generate mimicry on the part of the pupils, which in turn leaves an indelible impression on young minds. A clear penetration in the timbre of the teacher's speaking voice is needed: if the voice of the teacher is soporific the words seem to fall to the floor as soon as they are uttered, and the class goes wool-gathering.

A love of learning is a most desirable requisite in the good teacher. Versatility of approach to a lesson is important. Nothing stultifies children more than their ability to predict day after day how their teacher will approach a certain subject. This seems to contradict something else I have always believed, that the creation of a congenial monotony is a valuable part of a teacher's trade. I defend myself by stressing that once the fruitful monotony is achieved, the versatile departure from its norm is all the more dramatic. On the same level of approach, occasional informal language, such as is used in the home, is a welcome departure from scholarly routine.

I mention the importance of the cultivation of a sense of wonder when applied to the minor "epiphanies of the passing day." But I repeat that routine must have its place, for verbal or even physical buckjumping on the teacher's part often leads to bewilderment and mockery, especially if it does not come naturally to him. A well-read, rich personality, projecting himself or herself in the classroom, bears a marked resemblance to the fiction writer; both teacher and writer, if wise, will bear in mind that "everything, no matter how trivial, is grist to my mill."

There are so many teaching aids nowadays that I am tempted to question whether the use of the blackboard is a dead art in the class and lecture room. Not quite so, I tell myself whenever I watch television programmes that deal with current life in a school. A clear blackboard worker is someone I have always admired; most adults can summon up from memory the vivid image of a teacher who had this rare ability. Myself, I was impatient in this regard, but I do know that even the crudest use of sketching by way of illustration is not worthless.

In my deep-rooted opinion the teacher should, above all, act in harmony with the traditions and culture of the school area. Change in many aspects of local life is inevitable, or life calcifies and dies, but change, if it is desirable, should be brought about through the patient process of grafting rather than that of uprooting the known and replacing it with the unknown. Finally, under this heading, a teacher in class should learn to pace his energy and maintain economy of effort.

The generation of older teachers whom I knew as a young man were proud of their erudition. I recall one of these saying, "I am a philomath"—a lover of learning. The man spoke with a deep sense of pride. Nor did Latin and Greek come amiss to him and to many of his colleagues, which brings to mind an incident that happened to me in the local harnessmaker's shop.

A priest entered; laughingly I had occasion to use a Latin tag, to which he responded in kind. He left the shop, and then a schoolteacher entered; he and I conversed in Irish. After he had left an old traveller friend of mine came in, and under breath we carried on a desultory conversation in Shelta, the travellers' argot. During these proceedings the harnessmaker, a lovable character, remained silent. When he and I were alone he looked out the window and said dryly, "The priests have Latin, the schoolmasters have Irish, the tinkers have gammon—'tis only ignoramuses like meself speak English now."

Nowadays I find young teachers engaged in diverse local activities, all of which are praiseworthy; but since many teachers now live in towns and commute by car to school, the village schoolteacher is in danger of being a thing of the past. Proximity to the local second-level school, which mainly exists in the centre of a catchment area, is now a matter of importance to the teacher. Yet in future days, village domicile may provide a haven of peace from the growing stress of town traffic, and teachers may again return to live in the villages in which they teach.

So much for the teacher. A word or two on the parent, the third leaf of the scholastic trefoil.

A cross-section of the parents of schoolchildren in an average country town would include shopkeepers, farmers within the parish bounds, creamery and factory workers, teachers, doctors, bank and Government officials, members of the Garda Síochána, painters, contractors, garage proprietors, and mechanics. Tradesmen in the traditional sense of the word, such as smiths, saddlers, nailers, and shoemakers, are few and far between, although as a parent group they figured prominently in former times. How the teacher gets on with the parents is crucial for the school atmosphere. But it is foolish to think that he or she can satisfy every parent in the parish.

Parent power as an influence in school affairs is a comparatively new phenomenon in Ireland. In former years it did not exist in formal fashion, except perhaps in acute ad hoc situations. On reflection, perhaps it has always existed as an individual parent-teacher unit. That is where both parties trusted each other and had the welfare of the pupil at heart.

Is the management board a product of concerned parents, or is it the creation of ambitious individuals desirous of self-promotion or of limiting clerical power—a power that includes the hiring and firing of teachers?

Positions on the management boards of schools are highly prized in America. When treating of such a vast country it is foolish to generalise; however, in "mixed" areas it is natural that the Catholics would wish to be represented, as does the "WASP" (white Anglo-Saxon Protestant) segment. Semi-secret societies such as the Catholic Knights of Columbus, together with the John Birch Society, as well as the Freemasons, all see their presence on such boards as a useful activity with which to move society in a desired direction. Nor is the budding politician dilatory in this regard.

Consider a primary school of six or seven hundred pupils in a small town in the United States, or anywhere in the world for that matter. Let an aspiring politician find a place on the school board; he then has a platform from which to address possibly a thousand parents and voters. I hope that something like this type of careerism does not manifest itself in Ireland.

Certainly there is a sound reason for such boards in a metropolitan milieu, where traditional community coherence is often missing, but there is a need for vigilance in this regard in a small area where there is little elbow room. Recent enquiries I have made suggest that local school management, spearheaded by the parish priest or his delegated curate as chairman of the board, is working fairly well. However, I doubt if I could have endured it in its initial stages: no matter how democratic the despot (myself) may proclaim himself, I fear that change would have upset my schoolroom balance. I have always had a horror of committee members looking over my shoulder in the classroom, where, to my mind, the atmosphere should be an extension of that obtaining in the home. Above all I fear the future emergence of a sycophantic parochial teacher soft-soaping everyone and suppressing his or her real personality in the process. Where the board confines itself to helpful housekeeping, few problems arise; but the method of changing the school curriculum is through the ballot box.

I have heard nothing to better the verdict of a returned American experienced in such matters. "Where they're good, they're very, very good; and where they're bad, they're horrid."

Walking the streets of my native town over the years I came to know almost every parent of the children personally: a one-to-one board of management, in fact. This enabled me to resolve any schoolday difficulties having to do with the pupils. "I'm a parent myself," I would say. "Neither I nor any of the teachers will see your child wronged." I never knew this well-tested approach to fail. Our confidential talks would have to do with crises in the home, family illnesses, pending law cases, or the plight of an unemployed father.

If in the calm evening of a rough-and-tumble school day I realised I had unfairly punished a boy or hurt his feelings unduly, like any parent I suffered from remorse. I even went to the extremity of strolling in a part of the town I rarely visited; and on seeing the boy in question joyously playing on the street and greeting me as if nothing were amiss my heart rose in relief.

There are small hazards in one's contacts with the parents. Jealousy between neighbours regarding the progress of children often shows itself. Tact is called for where parents are estranged. One's knowledge of the locality is of help when a reading lesson extolling the bravery of a father must be conditioned in the presence of a boy whose dad has long since disappeared into the warren of an English city. Teachers have had to cope with the gospel according to Dr Spock filtered through half-baked programmes on radio or television. Not infrequently we have had to face educational jargon—"peer groups," "under-achievement," "cognitive variables"—that cause an old chalk-and-talk merchant like myself to murmur, "What use are these terms to me when I stand before a class?"

Parents who themselves are academically brilliant have difficulty in coming to terms with a child who fails to show the same prowess. Useless at times to say that the child has other gifts that will stand him in excellent stead as an adult—the ability to mix and be popular, for example. Nor does it convince them when the teacher mentions late developers, some of whom have astounded me and caused me to upbraid myself for missing out in my previous summing up of a child's abilities.

But all too often nowadays in the parent's mind there is anxiety regarding the future rat-race to secure entrance to third-level education. It is sad but true that the over-anxious parent is always projecting his child ten years into the future, with the consequent devaluing of a precious childhood.

Admonitions from parents heard over the years still echo in my mind. "Slap the fella next to him and that'll frighten him. He won't give any trouble then." "If you had nine of them to dress and feed you'd be late too." "Don't ever lay a finger on my child again." "He's wetting the bed with all this talk about Hell and punishment." Some of these I took to heart, others I ignored.

I cannot forget the visit of a small farmer at the school door holding a sturdy boy by the hand. After the preliminary greetings and the child's particulars given and taken, "You see him?" the man said, looking down at the lad at his side. "The winter morning he was born the doctor came up out of the room—a gruff, rough man that same doctor. 'Your wife is okay,' he said, 'but the child is gone.' Off with the doctor then.

"I went down into the room and looked at the blue infant. He seemed as dead as a doornail. The wife was out for the count, so I took the child up to the kitchen fire. I warmed the little body and rubbed olive oil all over it. There was no kiss of life that time. I massaged him, turning him this way and that. Heat, oil, massage for twenty minutes. The child suddenly gave a gurgle. He began to change colour. I worked away. A big belch and a cry—he was back from the dead. Here he is for you now, master, I leave him in your good hands."

So when I think of parents instead of pupils I am at the mercy of a host of memories that flick over like the pages of a picture book. I see a procession of heroic mothers who in times of deprivation struggled to feed, clothe and educate large families and keep up a face of respectability for their children's sake. I see an old woman in a shabby shawl standing on the pavement across the road from the school gate; for some reason I could never discover, she is searching the faces of the children racing past her. Day after day, there she stood. To this day it is a mystery to me.

Over all there are the ambitions of mothers being realised or abandoned; the boy they thought might be "priested" finishing up in trouble, and the reformed little rascal of the class well on his way to becoming a bishop.

And now I hear the gentle voice of a mother saying, "I was never here before, master, but I have a complaint..." A mother like this is always justified and should be respected.

In the middle of the most interesting lesson I have sometimes paused to look out the window at the hill above the town and ask myself what exactly I am doing.

Good God, I murmur, beyond that hill there are wonders to be explored: interesting men and women to be encountered, strange airs to be inbreathed, odd foods to be tasted—adventures of all sorts to be experienced and relished. What the hell am I doing here? Am I letting energy that should be channelled into writing escape through a waste-gate? The map of the world hanging on the wall could add to my mood of revolt.

When the melancholy was at its darkest, it was sometimes banished by the highly intelligent answer of a child, or a word of appreciation from a parent as, weary and drained, I walked home after school. I then realised that it is foolish to curse the dark; that we shall never evolve a perfect society; that I possess the world of literature at my fingertips to experience life in all its fullness—vicariously it may be, but nonetheless with a sense of perspective and deep satisfaction.

I smile then, somewhat wryly, and brace myself to get on with the bloody job, much of which is concerned with one of the great national idealistic goals.

CHAPTER NINE

The decision to include Irish as a school subject on the curriculum of the Free State leaned heavily on the older generation of teachers, of whom my mother was one. They had to start almost from scratch to master enough Irish to see them through the school day. This they did resolutely.

Both government and opposition professed a determination to restore the ancestral tongue. We younger teachers were then given five or more extra days free during the school year on condition that we had spent part of our summer holidays in an Irish-speaking area. The happiest days of my life were those spent in the Gaeltacht at that time. It was a revelation to find that Irish as a language was vibrantly alive in west Kerry, in Connemara, in the Aran Islands, and Ring. Hard to believe in the mood of today's Ireland that that was the rock from which the new state was hewn.

This idealistic approach the teachers of the twenties and thirties took with them into the classroom. In great measure they succeeded in what they set out to do. I can vouch for the fact that teaching the Irish lesson was one of the most enjoyable in the school day. Children of eight or nine, given a simple subject, could stand up and talk about it in Irish and with a sense of achievement in so doing. This was not an exception. From unbroken contact over a long period with other teachers, I know that what I say is true. Why then did the revival of the ancestral language not succeed?

The inspection system was over-rigorous. No idealistic goal can be achieved by fear: it must be inspired by a kind of dynamic or contagious love. The inspectorate contained many brilliant and understanding men, but there were among them those of parochial outlook who did not understand the profound nature of what was at stake; since they did not possess a vision, they were unable to impart one to others. The department to which they were answerable continued, more or less, to impose a system of examination with the attitudes of overlordship that had obtained in colonial days. Motivation was but dimly understood. Contrast the attitude of the Israelis, who fashioned a language out of shreds of vocabulary that existed only in the dustiest of vellum scrolls—an example of an idealistic solution to achieve an idealistic goal.

I still get blazingly angry when I recall the following incident. It was a bitterly cold day in winter during the years of the Second World War. The attendance at the old school was decimated by flu; I was left with a dozen or so ill-nourished boys huddled about a few smoking sods in a wretched fireplace.

The classroom door opened. A divisional inspector of schools entered. For once the early warning system of his arrival in town had failed.

Having signalled to the children to return to their places, he began to examine lads of nine years on the intricacies of Irish grammar. Having completely flustered and silenced them with these minutiae, he asked imperiously, using the abstruse conditional mood: "Dá bhfágfá barr na fuinneoige ar oscailt, cad a mhothófá ag teacht isteach?"—If you were to leave the top of the window open, what would you feel coming in? Receiving the laconic reply "Aer" from pupil after pupil, he scowled and demanded a more complete answer.

By now I had more than enough. Here were the the sick remnants of one of the best classes I had ever taught. In it were children who could gabble in Irish, as the saying goes, "till the cows came home." And here was an inspector who wanted to find out not what the children knew but what they did not know. Was it me he wished to impress?

For one of the very rare occasions in my teaching life, I decided to revolt. I called the inspector aside quietly and said under my breath, "Look at the sick children in this wretched school, most of whom should be in bed this appalling day. Look at the meagre fire around which they are huddled. And you come in to confuse them with esoteric cases of nouns and tenses of verbs. Let me tell you, sir, that if you and the likes of you are not checked you will give our beautiful language a grammarian's funeral."

He looked at me in astonishment. I don't think any pedagogic dog had ever barked back at him before. He walked quietly out the door.

To his eternal credit he made amends on a later visit. With great courtesy—it was a summer's day—he asked me to leave the class and walk up and down the playground with him, talking on a variety of subjects in which I found myself interested. He made no reference to our previous clash, nor did I. When he and I felt that the breach had been healed between us, we shook hands cordially and he took his leave.

The only book in Irish that in my extended experience the

children read, page after page, in advance of the class lesson was that humorous little classic that tells of an impish lad growing up in the Kerry Gaeltacht. I refer to *Jimín Mháire Thaidhg* by Pádraig Ó Siochrú, "an Seabhac." This book should have provided a valuable clue to the whole revival. Instead of the grammar-oriented textbooks there should have been a plethora of cheap storybooks with the accent squarely on the simple narrative story, to which children could respond. To me the more formal textbooks often conveyed the impression that the authors or compilers set out to indicate how resourceful they were in the use of the language, instead of seeing things from the angle of the pupil.

The emphasis, as we teachers found out rather late in the day, should have been placed on the oral side of the revival—on storytelling most of all—and we should have let grammatical accuracy remain in the background for a far later date.

By and large in this matter of revival we teachers stood alone. We were called "lá breás" for our pains, and were somehow depicted by the shallow-pated as antiquated figures. In public life as Taoiseach, and later as President, Éamon de Valera encouraged the use of Irish; but the main body of Dáil members—with some exceptions—seemed to regard the language as a joke, or a penance. Radio Éireann has some fine achievements to its credit, but to this day the outstanding personalities of radio and television shy away from using Irish, even in jest.

I personally have no axe to grind with regard to the media. Over the years I had my fair share of media exposure, but on a couple of rare occasions I have found it humiliating to be tipped off in advance to avoid breaking into Irish during a programme, something that as a true bilingual I have found hard to avoid. I am aware that it would be a breach of good manners to speak in one language if I knew the interviewer were not proficient in it. But the little anticipatory nudge rankled, especially when I found myself opposite a panel member to whom I had never spoken English. "Don't be incestuous now, yourself and X, during the programme," was the advice given. I knew what that meant, of course.

I wish I could convince the megastars of communication of the transcendent value of the national language, especially those who are already acutely aware of environmental perils. And I find it hard, on an occasion when Irish should be used, to accept excuses like "A Christian Brother turned me against it," or "I was belted for it at school."

Whatever sins I have committed during my school life, I have never punished a child for failure at Irish: I fully realised what was at stake. I wish I could convert certain important people to my viewpoint. After doing a crash course for a week or so they would be amazed at the welcome they would be accorded. But I will never be reconciled to the giggle of servility that so often greets the ordinary person's fortitude when he dares in public to speak a single phrase in Irish. Were it not for organisations like Comhaltas Ceoltóirí Éireann and the GAA we would long since have become mongrelised else-people—imitators to the last curl of our tails!

Anticipating the charge of being parochial or chauvinistic, I claim that I can hold my own against possible critics in any facet of English literature, which indeed is one of the props of my life and sustains me with a life of inner riches.

The power of the media sometimes stupefies me, and the mass mind it condones, which engenders an inability to think for oneself. Television for me is only a shadow of life: when someone "on the box" discusses the film world, what I see is the electronic feeding on the electronic in a further step away from reality. Is it to be wondered that at times, like the immured woman of the schoolbook poem, I complain, "'I am half sick of Shadows,' said the Lady of Shalott." But then I remind myself of the wonderful impressions conveyed by the television screen— to a limited extent one can vicariously travel the world while sitting in an Irish sitting-room. The trouble is to hold on to what is worthy in our own experience, and to maintain the dignity this implies.

Latterly I get the overpowering feeling that as a people we are being manipulated. I tend to query everything: the recurrence of an almost exclusively metropolitan panel of commentators; the editorial leaders calculated to defuse even laudable public indignation. And it seems to me that vested interests, mainly economic, even internationally so, are in unobtrusive control. When a crisis occurs that could well cause a little upset in Irish life, I try in advance to name the defuser. But as soon as my mind gets all worked up on the subject of manipulation, a heckling voice in my brain shouts, "Come to think of it, as a teacher, hasn't your whole life been devoted to manipulation?"

Some apologists step adroitly to one side by demanding an immediate and intensive study of Continental languages—a laudable aim indeed; but in so doing is it proper to make our ancestral tongue the whipping-boy of progress? Is it only a handful of people who nowadays appreciate the priceless gift that resides in the possession of a language that is truly our own? Fashioned over unreckonable centuries of adventure, passion, and agony, evolving to become a beautiful instrument with intricate systems of speech and writing, it is also capable of expressing and retaining every shade and syllable of emotion known to human experience. Those who label the revival of

Irish "a doomed diversion" are the real shortsighted ones among our people. They fail to see it as a powerful source of idealistic dedication, leading to solid achievement.

As I paced the classroom floor I was conscious of my antecedents who had used the language so superbly. I recalled the philandering Eoghan Rua Ó Súilleabháin, who employed it to seduce; Dáithí Ó Bruadair, who asked the Trinity to give his people better singing than he himself had given them; Aogán Ó Rathaille, the classicist, who complained not merely about the poverty that followed the overthrow of the native order but, what was worse, the insult that was the lot of the dispossessed.

As a subject, the teaching of Irish history is now very much in the news. Now, coals of fire are being heaped on the heads of the teachers of my generation. We are being blamed for the recurrent antagonisms of our country. Except for myself and a handful like me, the majority are not alive to defend themselves.

As I see it, the long and melancholy story of our adherence to the abstract idea of freedom is now being revised. I am compelled to ask myself if this is being done to keep history firmly in step with what some consider to be the political and economic welfare of Ireland.

Revised? It's being topped and tailed, neutered like an errant dog, rendered bland by being subjected to a type of scissors-and-paste collage to provide it with the coloration demanded by economic masters. Despite his plea for the common name of "Irishman" to be substituted for the various shades of religions and allegiances in Ireland, "Cut-throat Tone," as he has been named, is not now to be mentioned in polite circles. Pearse and other national leaders are relegated to a historical limbo.

So again I ask myself, why this revision of our national

history? Why are many of today's historians so hell-bent on revision? This phenomenon is not peculiar to Ireland. In every land, as the occasion demands, history is prostituted to serve current ends. And while small countries like Ireland are now condemned for even mentioning the heroism of their leaders of the past, great nations continue to proclaim the glory of their own story.

I quote from EL Doctorow, an eminent American novelist whose profound historical research is buttressed by a fine intellect and imagination:

> *I don't know of any responsible historian who would claim objectivity. They're all quite aware of the creativity of their enterprise. And what you decide is history and what isn't is tremendously subjective, but one of the reasons that history is being rewritten over and over is to satisfy the demands of the present. You write about the past in order to justify, rationalise or celebrate the present.*

My formal teaching of history was conditioned not wholly by what appeared in the textbooks but also by the human and vivid dimensions offered by folklore and the traditions of the ordinary people.

Standing on the steps of the church in Castletown Bearhaven, an old man said to me, "My great-grandfather stood here one Christmas morning in the 1790s and saw the masts of the French invasion fleet pass up behind those trees."

"How can you speak so confidently of that incident?" I asked an old man, the tradition-bearer of his locality, who had just described for me an incident that happened 250 years before. He drew himself up proudly. "Remember this," he said. "There are only twenty-five old men like me between you and the time of Christ." He went on to explain his statement. "An intelligent boy of ten speaking to an old man of ninety bridges a gap of eighty years. Put that old man back to the tenth year of his boyhood and again have him speak to an old man of ninety. Continue this process of reversal back the centuries, and with about twenty-five old men one is back to the time of Christ."

I recall the tale I heard in the Wexford area of the cursory burial of the croppy lads killed in battle in 1798, whose bodies where shovelled underground with a light covering of clay. The graves were unmarked; but with the passage of time the leather satchels of wheat grain they took with them germinated from the seam-split satchels and thrust upwards to mark the spot.

The truly human dimension to history and the value of the oral source was something that as a teacher I tried to convey to the children. So even in the teaching of history, everything is a story and a story is everything. History is far more than the daisy-chaining of dates and similar basic data: these constitute only the skeleton, needing the flesh of the imaginative incident to fill out its frame. Dared I then monkey around with a personal, bland version of Irish history that my young pupils, grown to manhood, would recall with amazement and possibly resentment?

The radio features by Donncha Ó Dúlaing tracing the retreat of Dónall Ó Súilleabháin Béarra were a most valuable exercise in humanising history. Events of almost four centuries ago were vividly brought to life by the descendants of the people who had greeted, or attacked, Ó Súilleabháin and his handful of soldiers and camp followers as they staggered through the snowy countryside on one of the epic journeys of Ireland.

For me this epic tale brought to life the bravery not alone of Dónall Cam Ó Súilleabháin and his followers but also that of old Ó Conchúir Chiarraí, whose slighted castle still stands at Carrigafoyle, near Ballylongford. The old chieftain resolutely staggered on and on; he thumped his ulcerated legs against a tree trunk to break the scabs and rid his sores of pus and blood. Doing so he cried out in semi-poetic apostrophe, "Legs that have borne me through the fall of Dunboy and the rout of Kinsale, do not betray me in this frozen countryside. Bear me up a little longer until we reach the hospitable castle of Ó Ruairc of Breffni, the last friend left us on earth."

Peripheral or perhaps central to an understanding of the history and geography of Ireland, as well as of the life of the ordinary man and woman, is a knowledge of native music, dance, and song. Many of the ballads of the Irish countryside are rough-hewn and, as it were, verbally adze-marked by honest craftsmen. Our store of folk song in Irish and English is one of the noblest treasures of our people.

Defiance of authority is a hallmark of much of our balladry. The authority is not necessarily that of a foreign government: it could be that of a cruel parent, a hiring farmer, a harsh landlord, or uncongenial circumstances, including unemployment, resulting in emigration and the leaving behind of a loved locality.

Our national ease in slipping into song, at times without preamble and as a substitute for the sharing of friendship, does not obtain in other countries: it is certainly foreign to even the younger generation in America and on the Continent, who demand a great deal of wooing before even joining in a well-known chorus.

As a boy I took piano lessons each afternoon for the best part of six years from a succession of music teachers. And all the while I could not come to terms with the piano. Sullen and obstinate, I continued to face the keyboard. At times I tried to identify the source of my distaste for that noble instrument. I was forced to the absurd conclusion that I rejected the piano simply because it could not be carried about in one's pocket to be played publicly at fairs, race meetings, and regattas. At that time all I lusted for was to listen to the ballads of the thronged market-place. A good ballad properly sung enthralled me.

My first formal music teachers were a venerable woman and her middle-aged niece. The pair were gentility personified. But they stood between me and the love of my heart: the wild music of the countryside. To me, these gracious women represented the tyranny of the tempered scale, while my grace-noted mind soared in the intricacies of a scale as old as the Celts themselves.

While the metronome wagged its pate on the piano top and the niece repeated "tafé-tafé-tá" while at the same time pointing to the notes with a wooden pointer, I sat there, my ear cocked to catch the words of a ballad being sung in the pub next door. As if suddenly realising that I had no idea what she was saying, my teacher rapped me sharply on my knuckles with the pointer. A stab of pain shot right up my arm. I reacted fiercely.

I stood up, grabbed my portfolio, and brought it crashing down on the head of the bishop's sister while at the same time I hissed the word "Bitch!" Then I raced for the room door, crashed it to behind me and, rushing home, locked myself into the water closet in the yard and refused to come out.

Hour after hour passed. The space at the top of the closet door offered a view of the stars and what appeared to be the face of an outraged moon. I was deaf to all appeals: these came mostly from my mother, for my idealistic father was then in poor health; I knew that if anything he was amused at the episode. "Come out, son. It's all right," she pleaded. No response from the rebel. Was she sobbing? At last she whispered in broken tones, "There's a black sheep in every fold. You're my black sheep." This got me. When she had left I crept up to my bed. The matter was never again mentioned in our house.

I still stuck to the ballad. No matter how naturally, even crudely, a ballad was fashioned, for me the balladmaker was "freedom's chanticleer." This love of the ballad I tried to convey to generations of schoolchildren.

I made dozens of such simple songs for my printer friend Bob Cuthbertson. When he had leftover piles of cut-off paper of all colours he would look at me and say, "Make a ballad to fit that lot." Armed with a quill pen and a cut-glass inkwell of violet ink, I set to work. Ambushes, rivers, famous greyhounds, dead hurlers and footballers, political upheavals, huntsmen and hounds, songs of love and hatred, of comedy and tragedy—all came alike to the quill pen. Later I scripted a Radio Éireann programme called "The Balladmaker's Saturday Night," which had a huge listening audience and helped an appreciation of the ballad to seep through the land. Ceoltóirí Chualann, Seán Ó Riada's famous group, received its first public performance in the Abbey Theatre when supplying incidental music for my play *The Song of the Anvil.*

All during this time, armed with a wire recorder, precursor of the tape recorder, I was scouring south-west Ireland in search of lost ballads. If I found an incomplete version I made up the missing verses. Such fine folk singers as Seán Ó Síocháin, Joe Lynch, Martin Dempsey and Nellie Walsh sang the ballads I provided.

Tiring of being known as "the Balladmaker"—for it was only one of the strings to my bow—through Mícheál Ó hAodha of

Radio Éireann I handed over the programme to such well-known people as Brendan Behan, Ben Kiely, Sigerson Clifford, Paddy O'Connor, and Pádraic Fallon. All in all it was great fun, and it certainly made an impact.

The approach to geography as a school subject has radically altered over the years, and now includes all kinds of subdivisions. It has a social side, a meteorological side, business facets of all kinds, migratory sideshows. Erosion, pollution and preservation now enter its ambit. It's a far cry from the parrot-like recitation of my schooldays: "Tullamore, Birr or Parsonstown, Banagher, and Edenderry."

What we possess by way of environment is becoming more valuable with every passing minute. We are now delicately balanced between holding and losing much that is priceless.

Until now I have placed little emphasis on the teaching of mathematics, apart from vaguely indicating that it is there. The primary school concerns itself with foundations, so I was content if the children had a clear conception of numeracy and a firm grasp of the addition, subtraction, multiplication and division tables. I kept telling myself that there had to be some interesting way to teach these monotonous processes apart from the choral singing of the tables (which I sincerely hope is still a feature of primary schools).

I divided the class of, say, forty into four teams of ten each. I tried to align the children in these teams with the areas traditionally serving town football teams. Each team elected its own captain and vice-captain. Pitting these teams against each other in various combinations of the tables, I found I could make progress.

What aroused most fanatical competition was a game called "Beat the clock." This involved filling a blackboard with a truly long tot, the addition of which I timed with a stopwatch. Giving the children a few days' notice, I would hold a competition to find the team with the fastest totting ability. I took the precaution of changing the bottom line of the tot after each team had finished. This competition concluded, and a little cup awarded to the winners, I would pick the two fastest totters from each team; this left me with eight lads to take part in a grand finale.

This caused feverish excitement among the boys. Each pair of finalists, surrounded by partisans, was trained to the last ounce in the parlours, stables and outhouses of the town. Eight tense totters tightened for the tally would face me on the appointed day. Some of the other classes, with their teachers, would be invited to come to my room for the occasion.

Here I am then, stopwatch in hand and about to let the champions race. A hush falls on the classes. "Go!" I say to the first lad as I press the button of the watch. Off he races. Six, ten, fifteen, twenty-three...feverishly totting like a bank clerk on Christmas Eve.

This competition would end in a blaze of excitement. The fastest of the fast was now pitted to race against the master—to wit, myself. If he beat me he would win ten shillings or a pound, I forget which. One of the other teachers would be called upon to time the event.

Over a period of several years I was beaten once or twice by young speed-merchants. These victors are now grown men; some are grandfathers. They still remind me of their famous victories.

Pounds, shillings, pence, and farthings. Tons, hundredweights, stones, pounds, and ounces. Gallons, quarts, pints, and measures.

When I reflect on the years of sweat spent driving home antiquated measures of this kind I still shudder. My hard-earned tables are nowadays reduced to an appliance held in the palm of the hand with a small panel of numbered buttons. It would not have irked me so much if I had not foreseen that decimalisation would simplify all the rote memory of money, weight, and measure.

Only at the outer and most advanced limits of mathematics is there an imaginative leap into the unknown, causing mathematicians to scribble formulas on the walls of bridges or to send missions into the unimaginable reaches of space. But this was not as yet in the province of the primary school. Despite the fact that a professor had once told me that a mathematical problem solved could be as artistically rewarding as a melody composed or a poem written, I remained prejudiced and unimpressed.

These then were the subjects—Irish, history, music, geography, and mathematics—and over the forty years my complete involvement in the small world of my classroom.

Browsing once in an old bookshop in England I came upon a book that gave me great pleasure and satisfaction. It was the unadorned autobiography of a French farm labourer of the last century. I hasten to stress that I draw no parallels between the teacher mentioned in its pages and my own experiences, except perhaps that one aspect of this book crystallised what I tried to do (as distinct from what I achieved).

The name of the book is *The Life of a Simple Man*; the author is Émile Guillamin. His experiences in late nineteenth-century France, especially those touching on rural customs, evoke a resonance in the mind of any reader familiar with a comparable level of life in the rural Ireland of the same time.

I take the following passage from the introduction by Eugene Weber, in which he makes reference to the author's school day.

> *Émile belonged to the first generation to enjoy free compulsory schooling introduced at the beginnings of the 1880s and he benefited from a teacher of that first generation for whom teaching was less a job than a calling. M. Beaune [the teacher] spoke seriously to them about serious things. Patriotism, human solidarity, the failures and hopes of humankind. He turned out 12 years' worth of young peasants marked by solid knowledge and the will to learn more. His influence persisted into the 20th century when we find his native village of Ygarande quicker to light it high street, to found Mutual Aid Societies, or libraries or education groups than any neighbouring village.*

Across the century that divides the dead from the living, I salute the ghost of Monsieur Beaune.

CHAPTER TEN

Thinking back on a lifetime spent mostly in a schoolroom, I find that there are two main sets of children that remain fixed in the foreground of my mind. Both sets belong to those who, from the point of view of society as it then existed, were considered marginal.

It was a cold night in midwinter, when the Second World War was drawing to an end. A friend had asked me to accompany him to the local railway station to meet a train.

A hoarse whistle in the distance announced the approach of the huffing and puffing steam train. A boy of eight or nine descended from a carriage carrying a small, cheap suitcase, and looked about him. A label was attached to the lapel of his jacket. My friend Éamon—the actor and storyteller Éamon Kelly, a member of the Save the German Children Society—went forward and read the label. "This is our man," he whispered.

I looked at the boy. Here was a child who had floated over land and sea from the conflagration of Europe. He was one of a number of children then accepted by foster-parents in many parts of Ireland. I have often wondered what the boy's thoughts were as he walked between two strangers through the murky streets of a town that for him must have been on the edge of the world.

Later, in the boarding-house where he was to stay for the night, he was made welcome before a warm kitchen range. When he had finished the meal we showed him upstairs to his bedroom. As he opened his little suitcase to put on his pyjamas we indicated that we would return later. We found him sitting up in bed. He looked at us and we at him. Tears began to flow down his cheeks. We didn't know what to say.

At the time I wore an Ingersoll watch in my breast pocket, attached to a strap that was anchored in the buttonhole of my lapel. Dangling the watch, I swung it by the strap, pendulum-fashion, before the boy's tearful eyes. He looked from one of us to the other. Suddenly he knuckled his eyes dry, and the slowest and warmest of smiles crossed his face. The natives were idiotic but friendly.

Many Kerry foster-parents had offered their homes as a source of refuge to these German children, and so, for us teachers, they constituted a pleasant interlude in school life. As principal of the school it was my duty to take their particulars when, led by their hosts, they attended for enrolment. With the help of a German phrase-book and their pidgin English I did the best I could to extract the requisite information. (The fact that the little pocket of German boys did have a language of their own was not lost on our own Irish schoolchildren.) In the classroom the German lads were obedient, dutiful, earnest, and honourable. They integrated well and were easy to teach. They had one other characteristic that I must mention: if they thought they were being wronged, or if a recommended course of action seemed to run counter to their sometimes obscure principles, they would dig in their heels. Then the blunt refusal to cooperate or obey was expressed by, "I von't. I von't!" They would continue quietly to protest their sense of wrong until the matter was put to rights—in a case like this it was prudent for the teachers to sidestep and not to confront.

One fair-day I had a visit from a sturdy German boy fostered in the countryside. He asked how his brother was behaving in school. I noticed a discrepancy between his surname and that of the brother about whom he had enquired. My question evoked a smile and the explanation, "There is a step, you see." His later greeting of his brother, whom obviously he had not seen for some time, was quite moving; I withdrew, leaving them together in the school hallway.

After a time I went out to see how the reunion was progressing. The elder brother whispered a final word of advice to the younger lad, who now returned to his classroom.

"He give you no trouble?" the visitor asked me.

"None at all—an excellent boy."

He then said, "There is no-vun but him and me. If he give trouble, I stop it."

"Everything is fine," I said.

As he left me he turned to explain his presence in town on that fair-day. This he did in the purest of Kerry dialect and intonation. "The raizin I am in town today is I sell an in-calf heifer for Paddy Sullivan the Councillor—you undershtand?"

I understood.

Ludwig, the turfcutter's son from the vast area of bogland near Hannover, found himself a home from home when he also helped to save turf with his foster-father just north of our town. He pre–sented himself at our school about twenty years after his departure. As he was now quite a man I failed to recognise him at first—this too in the presence of his fiancée, the lovely fräulein by his side. "I am Ludwig," he said; and I did my best to make amends. He and Gerda had saved up their money, he said, so as to visit Ireland before they married and to thank his foster-parents and teachers. The foster-parents must have been deeply gratified by the visit; I too reckoned it one of the rewards of a teacher's life.

Some time in the 1950s I heard on my old-fashioned Atwater-Kent radio that a severe storm was imminent. Listeners were warned to avoid falling trees and to tie down whatever of their outdoor property was loose.

The townspeople did as advised; let it come, the town was ready. Suddenly I recalled that there were a dozen or so travellers' caravans stationed in a boggy laneway about a mile from the town. What was worse, they were halted under a row of tall beech trees. I drove west to the halting site. "You're in a dangerous place under these trees," I shouted to the man tending a smouldering fire. "There's a storm on the way." The man looked up at the thrashing branches and said, "We'd better shift, so."

A hoarse shout and all was activity. Horses furtively placed in a nearby field were rounded up. I counted twenty-six children taking the place of the piebald horses as they put their shoulders to caravan wheels or hauled on the shafts of their "vargies." I took little part in the activity, as I was not sure if I was welcome. The work went on until all the vehicles were dragged to a safer site, where wheels were tied to the stout stems of whitethorn trees firmly rooted in the clay. I turned for home.

Up to this time these children, beyond a brief appearance for a week or two before First Communion or Confirmation, did not attend school regularly. They were constantly being moved on by the authorities. ("The outcast's fear of society is exceeded only by society's fear of the outcast.") Then, as they tended to settle, at least during the winter months—stealthily, as it were, and as a result of an important decision by one of the higher courts, which upheld the travellers' right to halt for the purpose of having their children educated—one by one, family by family, they entered the schools.

There are no social barriers between children; they are taught these by insensitive parents of insecure gentility.

About this time I had been chosen as chairman of a temporary local committee for the settlement of the travelling people. Unfortunately—or fortunately—I was on holidays for much of the hullabaloo that followed the building of three or four houses for the wanderers.

The lads I taught could, by ordinary standards, be called wild. As a rule they were not interested in the normal run of subjects, but if one took them aside and explained the importance of reading and writing they could be made to appreciate it. "You will be able to read the newspapers for your father and mother, write a letter home if you are away, read the posters and tell what picture is showing in the cinema—the whole world is open to you if you can read and write," I told them.

In the beginning these children were obsessed with the school toilets. (This happened in the new school.) This caused little surprise, since for centuries their forebears had had to use the roadside for their natural functions. But my lads seemed to treat the toilets as a source of amusement. One of them was constantly putting up his hand and shouting, "Can I g'out, master?" None of your "Bhfuil cead agam dul amach?" for him, nor even the genteel murmur of "T'ilet!" It took me some time to discover what he was at outside.

The other children kept complaining that all the enclosed

toilets, except the last one in the line, were occupied, and that the occupants refused to finish up and come out. I insisted that the children inside be given time. The complaints grew. "They won't come out, sir." I entered the lavatory and knocked at the door of the first cubicle, which showed the engaged sign. No response. Down the line of cubicles I went knocking at each door in turn, but with the same result. The crowd of waiting children grew still more impatient. A few of the boys then rushed out into the yard, "arrested" a travelling lad, and brought him back to me. "He did it," all yelled together.

The culprit smirked as he confessed what he had done and how he had done it. After entering the first cubicle, he had bolted the door behind him from the inside and proceeded, by climbing the partition, to repeat the process down along the line of cubicles, leaving by the door of the last one. The little rascal seemed in no way contrite for his transgression. I rebuked him, half sternly and half mildly.

Thereafter he was something of a school hero. He enjoyed his new-found status; with a group of admirers around him in the school yard he strutted like a gamecock. To me observing the town boys looking at him it seemed that they were jealous of their own failure to think of the trick. It took a newcomer, and a traveller to boot, to explore the adventurous possibilities of a new school building.

The background of many of these boys was well known to me. I could trace their lineage back to the faraway callers at our back gate looking for water as they encamped in the market on festive occasions such as the thrice-yearly big fairs and especially during the annual race meeting.

For one period in my life I was treasurer, organiser and letter-writer for the travelling people, writing often to the bishop "to separate their blood," the phrase used when cousins were about to be wed.

I went to the trouble of learning the secret language of the travelling people. It is known by various names: Shelta, Sheldru, Gammon, Cant, or even the Ould Nock—"the old thing." I learnt it because I wished to understand the traveller's mind and how it operated under shifting circumstances. Having mastered the basics I travelled to the west and introduced myself to the travellers there as a Kerry O'Brien (I was, after all, a Kerry Bryan) who had made "tomán gairéad floggin' waxy"—plenty of money selling linoleum. By this subterfuge I increased my vocabulary and recorded the leading "linguists." I studied Macalister's *Secret Language of Ireland* and found that the gammon had changed in certain instances since this store of words and phrases was recorded—indeed, it is always being changed in certain ways, with the aim of preserving secrecy. A subtle difference applied even between different clans. I once heard an old south-western traveller boast that no-one could "turn a corner" on him "even in a Galway gammon."

The gammon itself indicates a contribution from Italian (*parlary*), an intrusion from the cant of circus roustabouts (*tober*), and an odd word from Latin (*panis*), which buttresses Macalister's theory of the influence of homeless monks after the dissolution of the monasteries. These are not the only incursions: the language of masons—béarlagar na saor—and sixteenth-century English phrases like "Stow your whids" glisten unexpectedly.

But for the most part Shelta is cunningly fashioned from gammon Irish. The derivation of the word "scaihaab" for whiskey eluded me for some time, until I split the word into halves (between the *i* and the *h*) and rearranged the parts anagram-fashion. The solution was then obvious to anyone with a knowledge of Irish.

At the local convent a retired nun, an old friend of mine, was initially one of the teachers who undertook the task of teaching the girls among the travellers to read. Four times a year—for St Patrick's Day, Easter, Halloween, and Christmas—the girls, under the supervision of my nun friend, visited me in my school to show off their progress and prowess in reading. In the little staff room the nun and I sat in state behind a table while a crescent of girls of twelve or thirteen sat in front of us.

In the intervals of reading, some of them eyed me frankly. I was then conscious of the oddest frisson in their gaze. Since I was the first male teacher they had ever had, it struck me that they were sizing me up as a man.

One of the last lessons the girls read for me was about Michelangelo painting the ceiling of the Sistine Chapel. A more incongruous lesson for such pupils I thought it difficult to imagine; I revised this opinion on hearing them read with such aplomb. I then concluded that, owing to the vivid and volatile nature of their lives on the road, ever on the move, with sensation after sensation being the very stuff of their existence, it was no wonder they took the story of the master-artist in their stride: not even this sublime subject was alien to their innate perceptions.

Little prizes were bestowed on the girls with all the pomp and ceremony Sister and I could muster. Their appreciation was implicit in their shy reply, "You're good, master; thanks."

The boys saw no danger. One proved to be a fine Gaelic footballer, and received the prize as the best player of the year. I met him again a year or two ago in the west. Now a grandfather, his face showed the hard marks of the road, yet he glowed with pride when I recalled for him his hour of fame. This fearlessness often spilled over into a faked truculence; at playtime, I sometimes heard voices raised in dispute over chestnuts or marbles, and noted the half-pulling of the jacket off the shoulder as a sign of challenge to a fight.

Tragedy, in its major and minor forms, was never far from the lives of these boys and girls. One of the boys lost an eye when dashing through a thorn thicket. There was another little lad, among the gentlest and most sensitive boys I ever taught, a half-traveller who took after his tattooed grandfather, who, despite the exigencies of war and homelessness, was a gentleman to his fingertips. If one of his brothers gave trouble this boy would approach me quietly and whisper, "He's not tratin' you right, master." Once he said, "If I'm bould, bate me, master." Not for the world would I have laid a finger on him. I saw him as a gentle pioneer who would act as an example to others; not alone was he obedient and sensitive but he was also highly intelligent in class. It was this boy that I saw drowned on the river bank; my grief was inconsolable.

The travellers' graves are just inside the gate of the graveyard that adjoins the school playground. The graves are festooned with necklaces and dolls; there is even a miniature caravan to remind the dead of the rough but vivid life they have led. A great timber Rosary beads, probably the gift of an elderly monk, hangs from one of the crosses, and, swaying in the breeze, at times it rattles against the stone. The flowers, artificial for the most part, and the piling of gewgaws puts one in mind of certain aspects of South American Catholicism. The word *accident* cut in the nearby grave markers also reminds the observer of flat carts or motor vans driven at reckless speed through a darkened countryside. The headlong nature of their lives all too often ends in fatal accidents.

I learnt many valuable lessons about the travelling people. There is a period of the year, about the end of March or the start of April, when the rover's patience often snaps and he is subject to inexplicable outbreaks of anger. This time of year marks the end of what has been more often than not a miserable winter of rough living out of doors.

Give the average house dweller even two or three days' living under such harsh conditions—in the old days it meant a wet straw bed, leaking canvas, smoking fires, and no toilet or washing facilities—and at the end of such a penitential period the chances are that he will not be on his best behaviour. In my dealings with adults and children of the travelling people I was extra cautious at this time of year.

Twice I forgot to exercise this care; on both occasions it almost cost me my life. My unguarded reference to the fine silver-mounted riding-crop he was carrying was misconstrued by a traveller who may have thought that I was a "shidogue" or garda. As I turned away I read a sudden warning written on the face of another of the clan. Spinning on my heels I was just in time to see that the owner of the crop, holding it by the lighter end, had it raised on high and was about to crash it down on my head. On seeing my face he froze, lowered the riding-crop, and turned away.

Times have changed. Many of our erstwhile charges have grown comparatively affluent on the sale of antiques, which they identified as they raked the countryside. Their mid-Munster confrères—there are many social gradations of their clan system— own splendid houses on the hill off the Main Street of Rathkeale, proving thereby that the incredible can happen in the course of a generation or two. Twenty years ago I prophesied that a member of the homeless folk would be ordained a Catholic priest. My informants tell me that it has come to pass.

"Are you okay for a colour telly?" shouts the weather-hoarse voice from the Hiace van. "You taught me, so I owe you that much." As he changes gear he adds with a laugh, "I was right bould then. You should have belted me well. Goo' luck, master!"

On the occasion of the First Communion day I selected a travelling lad for the honour of reading from the brass lectern on the altar steps. It was a time when there was some local friction about the housing of the travellers, and eyebrows were raised. He was a fine, strong reader with a certain magnetism in his voice, and he completed his task to perfection. I shall not easily forget his declaiming in clarion tones a line taken from one of the earliest disciples: "It is not because of my people that I wear the badge of shame." Standing beside him as he read, I knew the words had real meaning for all present.

There's a great to-do in pious Ireland about the "prayers learnt at the mother's knee." Any experienced teacher will tell you that this is largely a myth. I stress the word "largely," for there are exceptions. The travelling children always had a sketchy knowledge of the commoner prayers, even in the old days when they rarely darkened the door of a school. They were taught the prayers by the fire on the roadside, simply because they provided a formula for successful "gayging" or begging. The Lord's Prayer does exist in gammon; although I have never heard it recited, it was recorded long before my time, and again lends support to the Macalister theory of the homeless monks.

The out-of-school version of the prayers was gabbled, confused, and inaccurate. It was aimed mainly at the "cunnick" or priest encountered on the road. The first question the priest invariably asked the lad or lassie with the extended hand was,

"Can you bless yourself, child?" The child did so at breakneck speed. Then, "Have you the Lord's Prayer?" This was recited also at speed, with the most unusual interpolations and mispronunciations. However, as often as not this satisfied the clergyman, who invariably rewarded even this rude manifestation of piety.

Within the confines of my noisy mansion I often watched these resilient lads and wondered what the future held for them. Some fell by the wayside: when old ways die and new ways have not yet taken root there is a gap of danger, exemplified throughout the world in similar situations.

I have no illusions about the perceived romanticism of life on the roads. It is a rough life and takes a tough type of person to cope with it. But despite overwhelming odds, the travellers have managed to survive. Taking refuge in alcohol must be judged in the light of appalling living conditions.

I made one of the great discoveries of my life as a result of my dealings with "God's gentry." I received a cablegram from *Natural History*, a distinguished New York journal published by the American Museum of Natural History, asking me to write an article on the Irish "tinkers." I did so at once. It did not entail a great deal of trouble, as I had been carefully noting details for years. In the article I told of Shelta, of the probable origins of the homeless people, and of their superstitions and religion, ending with some kind of projection of what the future held for them.

In sending me a copy of the journal containing the article the editor enclosed almost a hundred offprints or reproductions of the article, adding that I could expect to receive requests for copies from various quarters interested in such subjects. I had no idea what I was letting myself in for.

Day after day I received postcards from far-flung countries soliciting a copy of the article. Presently my initial store of copies was exhausted. All this fuss I found incomprehensible. Why were so many universities in so many countries interested in a subject that, at the time, I considered was of Irish interest only?

On receiving a belated request, this time from the head of the Biology Department of an American university with which I once had contacts, I wrote back introducing myself and asking the reason for the international commotion. Here is a summary of the reply I received:

In view of the possible annihilation of the human race by nuclear weapons, the manner of survival of marginal tribes who have spent their lives in areas of harsh environment over an extended period has become of compelling interest to governments throughout the world. The fact that the Irish tinker has survived for centuries, living at times in makeshift tents on the road edges under the inhospitable conditions imposed by a climate subject to considerable rainfall, has become of significant importance to the governments of various countries. Among those tribes being researched are the Inuit, the Lapps—and the Irish tinkers.

I read this with increasing astonishment. And looking at the impish faces of the travelling lads, I addressed them mentally as follows:

You are far more important than you could imagine in your wildest dreams. Survival—that was the name of the game. And how have you survived? By never missing a trick. By solving the problems of living as posed by each new day. By recalling the old proverb that comes down from the Famine times: "God help the rich, the poor can beg." By sharpening one's wits to a razor's edge. By flattery and wheedling. By raising one's voice from the camp-fire to ask, "Wha' time is it, sir?"—not because you wished to know the time but to learn whether the voice of the passer-by could be that of the owner of the field into which your piebald horses have been driven for the night.

You have survived by cashing in on the irregular and sometimes seasonable demand for apples or asses, for shamrock or camphor balls, for Sacred Heart badges or linoleum; you have lived by cleaning latrines, sweeping chimneys, bottoming cans, and mending umbrellas, and then replacing an outworn trade by learning about Queen Anne tables as you once learnt about the hooves of horses.

Thinking of the ancestors of my classroom travellers, I cannot forget the grandfather of the tribe, the King of the Clan, Charlie, who served in the trenches in the First World War. Having captured a village, this then young man, a survivor from birth, made straight for the hen-coops of the French farmhouses, wrung the necks of half a dozen pullets, and then, wearing his skirt of dead chickens slung from his belt, walked along the top edge of the trenches singing out, "Anyone there from Listowel?" On finding a soldier from our neighbourhood he would bestow part of his feathered booty and shout, "That's a present from home!" It occurs to me that he could well have been firing his rifle at the grandfathers of my German pupils.

That same old man I see now as he neared his end, lying in a pool of animal urine for nights on end, and waking to strip his teeth and snarl defiance at those who would have him move on. What can break the spirit of a man? Rise up, old ghost of a traveller. For me, if for no-one else, you have earned your place in the noble mosaic of human endurance and survival.

My traveller children are all now grown up and presumably able to read what I have written. I trust that if they do read my novel and play *The Honey Spike,* which depicts traveller life in all its joys and horrors, they will be able to appreciate the spirit in which I have written about them, and that they will feel interested and even proud of the colourful life of their elders, and above all that they will not see me in the role of an amused patron.

These special groups in the school experience must be viewed as exceptions against the backdrop of the other children, among whom were many boys of foreseeable brilliance. It would be invidious to isolate these by naming them, but they were certainly there. I watched them become adults—and yes, in almost all cases, they fulfilled the fine promise of their boyhood.

CHAPTER ELEVEN

I boarded the SS *United States*, then the world's fastest and most modern liner, at Southampton in June 1963, one of a group from many countries who were to attend an international seminar at Harvard University, where we were to spend almost two months under the directorship of Henry Kissinger.

In a period of seven or eight weeks we were to experience a cross-section of American life in almost all its strata. The sample of participants already on board ensured an exhilarating clash and confluence of cultures.

From Nigeria came Adolphus, a dignified Ibo; from Sri Lanka came Robin; from Norway came Lars, who later became a valued friend; and from England came Eric, an unusual and original man whose love of poetry knew no bounds. There were numerous others. Ireland had two representatives, in the persons of Denis O'Sullivan (Denny Owen), then chief whip in the Dáil of Fine Gael, and myself.

To the seasoned traveller of today, when even schoolchildren travel to European destinations on Easter holidays, my journey will seem old hat, but I had been only once or twice on a liner or steamship before, and that was to the Continent, mainly to

Cherbourg or to Esbjerg in Denmark, in addition to a crossing or two of the Irish Sea. A transatlantic liner was a different matter.

It was a hot, hot summer. There was a feeling of claustrophobia, accentuated for me since I shared an inside cabin—one without a porthole. I know exactly how office workers feel in some of the office buildings when they cannot open the windows. As we neared the middle of the Atlantic the heat in the inside cabin grew intolerable. I spent most of the nights sitting in the companionway outside, wearing only the lightest of pyjamas. Others did the same. It made me wonder what it must have been like to experience the summer crossing in a coffin ship during the Famine.

I began to enjoy a tentative sense of companionship and adventure with the others on board, but relief for me came in an unusual way. "I've been searching the ship for you," shouted Denny Owen as he burst into my cabin. "Hurry or you'll be late." "For what?" "There's a competition for folk songs going on for the past hour in the main lounge. Some of our friends have sung. The whole passenger list is taking part. Don't let oul' Ireland down! Hurry!"

To my own amazement I found myself convinced that I should compete. A quick dash to my cabin and the donning of an Aran geansaí and a woven crios and I was ready for the fray—and as caparisoned and as ethnic as anyone on board! Presently I was on stage, microphone in hand. I explained briefly the story of a crazy billy-goat who attacked in turn the law and the cloth, both of whom thought him the devil incarnate. I then launched myself into "An Poc ar Buile." Holding the high note of "Aililiú," I gave it the works, and in a lather of sweat I handed back the microphone and headed for the upper deck, there to commune with the great span of sea and the god of insomniacs. I was just nodding off when Denny came rushing onto the deck and shook me awake. "You've won!" he shouted.

Folk singers of America, I declared, here I come! I slept. I woke in time to go on deck and view the sentimental but emotional representation of freedom that was the Statue of Liberty. Steel spiders were busy spinning the cables of a new bridge. There, as I had pictured them a thousand times, were the tall walls of Manhattan. The air was hotter than the halls of Hell.

In the seven weeks that followed we were exposed to a richness of experience from some of the finest minds of the American continent, without any political orientation whatsoever. It seemed as if a great deal of what made up the United States was compressed and placed before us for examination. Of the forty or so participants almost twelve were in the humanities or literary group and the rest in the political and economics group. For me, exchanging views with these participants was like entering an Aladdin's Cave of wonders. Before long I found myself hyperstimulated.

I started off with an advantage or two, as I was known to some of the course lecturers through my stories. For a writer to proclaim that he is not an egotist is a contradiction: it is his trade and mission to get others to view events through what he is convinced are his own unique eyes. The scribbler who declares the opposite is a hypocrite or a fool.

The lectures political, literary and economic were on the highest possible level. They ranged over such subjects as urban renewal, labour relations, the Japanese economic recovery, literature in south-east Asia, experimental films, and the British dilemma. To this were added visits to theatres, museums, factories, radio and television studios, law courts, prisons, and deprived areas, and many memorable excursions.

But what I appreciated most were the literary meetings and lectures: talks on the staid cadences of Henry James, the American European, and on the electric flourishes of modern writers displaying what our own Pádraic Fallon called "the shorthand of the nerves." I packed in all the poetry I could with a view to regurgitation in the long winter nights at home; it would then be "emotion recollected in tranquillity."

The open-stack bookshelves of Widener Library were mine to explore; with this embarrassment of riches I coped as best I could. The later Yeats was everywhere to the fore: a reading of "Byzantium" at night can still keep me awake for hours. Sometimes our arguments on world literature or world politics went on until the small hours in the cafés around Harvard Square or on the steps of Holworthy Hall. I didn't care if I never went to bed; even if I retired early I couldn't sleep. Heat was the single serpent in our paradise. I continued to swim in sweat during sleepless nights punctuated by numerous cold showers.

Again and again in the long reaches of the night I asked myself why I had come to America. I had come, I answered, to get away from the beloved claustrophobia of small-town Ireland, and from a distance to sum up what was important in my own culture. I soon found out that as far as Massachusetts was concerned, dodging Ireland was completely out of the question.

The Irish presence was everywhere; its influence was both pervasive and powerful in the Cambridge and Boston area. The sons and daughters of Irish parents were a revelation. Poised, educated, reserved, confident—the young professional men and women were proud of their parents' struggle to give them the best education possible.

This brings me to the two most important statements I learnt in this and subsequent visits to the university life of the United States. The first advice was, "Keep an opening to the left." By this was meant not merely to tolerate the political opinions of those who carried the credo of socialism to the extremities of communism, but also to be slow in condemning any movement welling up from the ordinary people. Often incoherently expressed, even outrageously so, its passion—and this extends even to literature—possesses a natural dynamic that embodies the seeds of renewal. "The right finds itself with its back to the wall: it has cut itself off from freedom of choice," was an extension of this statement. I continue to test modern developments with the litmus of this advice. If I do not always fully embrace certain conclusions, I try to isolate the precious twenty per cent of value implied by far-out statements and stances. If an extreme and intolerable position results, the remedy—at times by internal combustion—is inherent in the system. So those who pigeonhole me as a frozen conservative are mistaken.

The second revelatory statement went somewhat like this. The American dream is crystallised in much of what has been written by Mark Twain. When the going becomes rough, when the odds against the individual spirit become overpowering, one makes a raft and floats down the great river to start life anew where the grass on the river bank seems green and inviting. Add to this the frontier resource of self-reliance—and there in a nutshell is the adventurous spirit of the United States.

If this ethos is for export, it means that everyone should have a hideaway of the mind, a place to pole his raft ashore, an escape hatch even if it were never opened, but always a (possibly imaginary) means of starting life afresh, a mooring of sustenance to be used in the extremity of personal anguish. How to transfer this philosophy of living to the small island of Ireland where there is "great hatred, little room," where jealousy can be acutely personal, where we resemble caged budgies each issued with a bell, a mirror, and a miniature ladder to climb, is quite a problem. But I am buoyantly hopeful that the theory is valid, even on our small scale.

Get away from Ireland and from all things Irish? Look back with objectivity to find what is significant on many levels? I tried to follow this line of thought, but not for very long. In the milieu in which I enjoyed a brief existence it seemed, if anything, that the minutiae of Irish life were enlarged under the magnifying glass of racial nostalgia. So, as gracefully as I could, I abandoned the attempt to be objective.

Anything could happen in the United States. On one occasion, when visiting with other delegates a public school, from a gallery in a lecture theatre I overheard a story of mine being teased and dissected for the first time. Up to that time I had only the faintest idea of the impact of a story on a live audience. My story "The Cat and the Cornfield" tells of a cat who betrayed its master, a parish clerk, who had lured a tinker girl into a cornfield. Nemesis in the shape of a parish priest armed with a blackthorn stick stood on the roadway. Now my virtues and deficiencies as a short-story writer were under scrutiny. I felt like a patient lying on a bed in a teaching hospital when the specialist lectures his students on my particular disease, referring to me as if I were solely an object placed there to illustrate symptoms of a malady about to be diagnosed.

Would the future recollection of just this incident and its audience reaction alter my approach to stories yet to be written?

Would I be bent towards tailoring tales to suit a particular readership? I was conscious of the fact that by my presence in these gracious surroundings I was illustrating a reconciliation of disparates much as I had, I hoped, always tried to achieve in short fiction.

Why this reaction, I probed further within myself. Once again the image of myself in my teaching role, armed with a small rusted coal shovel, collecting the afternoon faeces in my lousy school hovel, seemed too incongruous to be mated with the elegant surroundings in which I found myself. As I led the way back to the waiting coach I realised that not only was I being forced to look over my shoulder at Ireland but in so doing I was also compelled to look deep into myself through the clear glass of far better conditions than those I experienced at home.

Finding ourselves with a few hours to spare in our busy schedule, Denis and I went to see an Italian Restoration play in a local theatre. It was dark where we were seated. Having entered the theatre without planning it and wearing only shirt and trousers, we had asked at the box office for seats at the rear of the gallery— theatregoers in America dress somewhat formally. Suddenly a young woman with vivid red hair made her entrance onto the stage. I gave an involuntary gasp. Every gesture of her hands, every movement of her body, reminded me of someone I knew. But who?

Awaiting my opportunity, I left my seat and held the open programme under a dim light. The name given for the red-headed woman was Étaín O'Malley. Immediately a series of images flashed through my mind. I seemed to see a young medical student, also red-headed, lying between railway sleepers during the Easter Rising and firing vaguely in the direction where he thought the British forces were. I then saw a pattern of half-horseshoe marks on the same man's battered face to indicate where he had been beaten with rifle butts in Dublin Castle. A small-town barracks I saw in flames, and later I saw a pall of smoke hanging above the blaze of the Four Courts during the Civil War.

More personal to me was the terror that had gripped me on the die-straight stretch of the Listowel–Ballybunion road when the same red-haired but now middle-aged man at the wheel of a car in which I rode drove straight for a narrow gap between two cars and got through by a whisker, the while I clutched his forearm in abject fear. That was Ernie O'Malley—an outstanding figure in the War of Independence. Later still I saw him when he had come to stay with us during the local race week, a sodden sleeping-bag in hand, turning the key in my front door early in the morning and saying, "Pretty damp out there," as I showed him to the bedroom that had awaited him since the night before.

When the play had ended I went to the stage door and asked for Miss O'Malley. "Yes?" she said sweetly when she appeared, the greasepaint not fully wiped off her face. I looked straight into her eyes. "You're Ernie O'Malley's daughter?" I asked rudely. "Who are you?" she asked. "A friend of your father's." I wasn't allowed to get away after that. Denis and I chatted with Étaín for a long while. About Ireland, what else?

The Irish consul-general in Boston is quite an influential person and provides a strong link between the Irish in Massachusetts and those at home. While I was there the then consul-general, Gearóid Ó Cléirigh, invited me to join himself and his wife one Sunday at a private beach some miles north of Boston. In my swimming togs and lying full length beside my hosts, I could well have been in Ballybunion but for the fact that the day was much hotter.

We were chatting about traditional music when I raised myself on my elbow and glanced back at the elegant hotel commanding the beach. Referring to its air of opulence, its parasols and swimming-pool, I said idly, "It must cost a pretty penny to stay there."

Overhearing this remark, a huge man lying sunbathing on a mat quite close to us rolled over and, addressing me, asked, "What did you say?"

"I said it must be quite expensive to stay in that hotel," I replied.

Whereupon the man said cryptically, "Not with that accent, it won't."

"What do you mean?"

"Just what I say. Go up and ask for George. Tell him to give you the vacant penthouse. Stay there as long as you wish. Free."

"How can you make me this offer?" I asked.

"I own the joint."

"There must be some catch in it."

"A catch? Sure. Not a big one."

"Let me hear it."

"Today is Sunday. Take possession at once. Nothing to do till next Saturday."

"And then?"

"George will drive you to a bungalow in the Catskills. There you'll find an old lady in a bed. Talk to her all day about Goddam Ireland. Sing about it if you like. Talkin' about Ireland is the only thing that makes her happy."

"The old lady is...?"

"My mom. Irish-born. I'm mighty fond and mighty proud of her. But I gotta attend to business in various places. Interested?"

I had picked up an American idiom that refers to the tickets issued when a ball game is washed out by rain. "Can I have a rain-check on that offer?" I asked with a smile.

"Sure," he said. "With one proviso. My mom hasn't got a rain-check on life."

More than anything else, what delighted my heart was to see how the immigrant Irish, when presented with an opportunity to better themselves, more often than not through education, gripped it firmly, and prospered. I met middle-aged women, poised and self-reliant, who had come out from Ireland as servants and who by attendance at night classes had eventually qualified as doctors.

I was talking to an Irishman wearing work-stained dungarees when, after a few minutes' chat, he invited me to Sunday dinner with his family. Noting how my eyes unworthily fell on his soiled garments, he softly said, "Never mind my old clothes— wait till you meet my family." I accepted at once. I was in for a surprise. Superbly balanced and impeccably dressed, his three sons, all professionals of the highest calibre, listened with keen attention to their father and myself as we gossiped about Ireland. Implicit in the welcome by young Irish-Americans was a sense of gratitude to the older generation, who were still proud of their origins.

The phrase "the land of opportunity" for me now began to assume its full meaning. I was conscious also that in minor measure this progress of our people abroad could be paralleled at home in Ireland. For me especially it seemed that the seed of personal fulfilment could be made to germinate in the minds of schoolchildren. How to stimulate its growth? If I could answer this question to my satisfaction it would have been worth while travelling to America. And enduring its heat.

The Irish are everywhere in the United States. Though their links with home are weakening, they are now a people of power and education. Our literature and the noble work of Dr Eoin MacKiernan have already provided us with a bridgehead. In moments of tragedy the generosity and loyalty of the Irish-Americans to their own is most praiseworthy.

The thought struck me forcibly that we had made only sporadic attempts at welding the American Irish into a coherent organisation, one that could speak with authority and act in unison whenever the well-being of the Irish homeland needed it. The Ancient Order of Hibernians came closest to the attainment of this ideal. Organisations like the Friendly Sons, minutemen of different kinds, the various political and benevolent county societies and the numerous ad hoc societies organised for St Patrick's Day dinners can hardly reassure us that as a people we have reached even one-tenth of our potential in this regard.

I say this not without a sense of trepidation and a feeling of awe at the magnitude of the task that confronts those who would undertake a mission that could arouse the fiercest jealousies among the Irish-Americans themselves. Successive governments seem afraid to help or lead in this regard. Granted that if they ventured to do so they could create a Frankenstein monster. But every worthwhile movement involves risk.

When responsible Irish-Americans address themselves to the recurrent agony of Ireland, the response of the average Irish politician is as follows: "They're out of touch in America. They see Ireland at a safe distance; their viewpoint is conditioned by shamrockery, balladry, sentimentality." Privately they add, "If we must keep touch with Irish America let us do so at gold-plate dinners and on the conservative level of affluence. Money is cautious. Moneyed people seldom rock the boat." Not for a moment do I decry the value of "putting one's money where one's mouth is," but it must be kept in mind that money cannot buy everything.

It may be salutary to consider that when an Irish-American spokesman speaks his mind he may be commenting from his experience of a free country. How long it will remain so is a moot question: as a lover of the United States and its people I tremble as a friend trembles when I read of it adopting the role of policeman to the world. Meanwhile my dreams of Irish-American constitutional power must possibly await an hour of crisis in Ireland and for the appearance of a leader worthy of that hour.

I could have remained on in America, at considerable profit to myself. I found myself welcomed to the full by the king-makers of Massachusetts, who had arranged an unofficial meeting with President Kennedy in a homely kitchen where he dropped in for a chat and a cup of tea. Because of the death of the President's son the informal appointment was cancelled. Did I wish to meet other personalities, some of them of immense power in the land? Honestly, I did not. Home was calling. I was grateful for the fine experience, but I wanted to return to Ireland.

I had plenty to think about as, with my international friends, I leaned on the ship's rail and watched the Manhattan skyline recede. There had been a farewell party in our cabins, given by some of the Boston Irish.

In my mind I flicked over the main events of an exciting period of my life: my first visit to the United States. The most disparate thoughts floated to the surface of my mind. I coped as best I could to make sense, and use, of them. "Ah, well," I told myself, "I have all winter to reduce them to coherence."

On boarding ship I had acted on a shabby impulse. I went straight to the purser and changed my cabin so as to have a cabinmate other than Eric the Englishman. I did this in the interest of sanity. When he chose to recite poetry, and he had a voluminous knowledge of it, he almost trepanned me with sheer excitement, so that it resonated and detonated in my head for days. He knew I had changed cabins and why I had done so; it caused him much amusement that his voice could exercise such power over me.

The remnants of our international group were still together, bound for various destinations in Europe and Asia. After a while life on a liner, which is really a sumptuous hotel on water, becomes claustrophobic. Closer to the homeland there were the usual Irish ballads, with some of us chanting John Locke's "The Exile's Return." We kept looking across the black-and-white water scudding in the early hours of the morning to catch the first lights of the Irish coast. Others on deck had transistor radios pressed against anything metal so as to hear perhaps the inspired yelping of Mícheál O'Hehir renewing the excitement of the day's championship matches from Croke Park.

As Kerry pushed its grey headlands out to meet us, I had to answer a question I had already shoved to the back of my mind but which sooner or later I had to face.

Before my departure Bill Murray of Clare, then lecturing in the English Department of a college of the State University of Iowa, told me that he had heard on the jungle drums of literary Irish-America that I had expressed a desire to visit Iowa City. (Under his full name, William Cotter Murray, Bill later published a fine novel, *Michael Joe*, based on his boyhood experiences in west Clare, later serialised on Radio Éireann.) If this desire still held, I might like to know that Vance Bourjaily, an important writer and lecturer in the International Creative Writing Program, was taking a six-month break—and if I applied to be appointed visiting lecturer in his absence I had a good chance of being successful. The Iowa course, headed by the famous Paul Engle, was among the very best in the United States.

But again I asked for a "rain-check": I had to return home, think things over, and possibly persuade my patient wife to travel with me to the cold mid-west of America early the following year. I had also to make other family arrangements, even though four of my sons were qualified, two in law, one in secondary teaching, another in the civil service—the youngest had yet to finish his law examinations. I had also to take soundings in the Department of Education about whether I would be released from school duties if I paid a substitute in my absence. This was a concession then rarely granted. Bill agreed to await my decision. I wondered if at that late hour—I was then fifty-three—I was beginning to have a love affair with the United States.

As the liner entered Cork Harbour and the tender came out to meet us it was a cool, grey morning with a rawish wind blowing into our eyes. There was old Cóbh and the spire of St Colman's. I was late in the queue seeking the solace of a cup of Irish-brewed tea, so when my turn came I was served it in a slapdash fashion. The woman in charge had to drain the dregs of several set-aside teapots before she squeezed out a cupful so strong that one could trot a mouse across it. Nettled by this, I unguardedly remarked, "I know I'm back in Ireland when I get the dríodar of pot and bottle." The woman turned on me like fury. In her best Coal Quay accent she shouted, "The cheek of you, you bastard! You mightn't have had an arse to your trousers before leaving for America, and you come back to us now full o' bullshit and grumblin' about the colour o' your tea!" I meekly bowed my head and suffered the colourful rebuke.

My family met me when I had cleared the customs. When we had driven a few miles along the road to home my wife and son gently broke the news that my elder brother Jack had died suddenly and had been buried during the period of my voyage home. Jack was a pure scholar, loving scholarship for its sake and with little thought of publication. His entire teaching life was spent in a primary school in what perhaps was the most deprived area in Dublin. Firsts in MA and the old King's Scholarship examination for entry to training college could certainly have gained him promotion, had he so wished, but whenever I broached the subject of change he would counter with, "It's there I'm wanted most."

My loss was tiny compared with that suffered by his wife and young family. It took me some time to come to terms with sadness suddenly superimposed on excitement and joy.

CHAPTER TWELVE

Back again to Ireland in time to savour the season's end at home: the All-Ireland finals, the races, and the inevitable return to the schoolroom; but as yet I had not got time to sift my impressions.

The period leading up to my return to the United States—the end of 1963—was a particularly troublesome time for me physically. Prone to kidney stones—a stone-maker I called myself—on my return to school I began to suffer the complaint in acute form. When the pain was at its worst I had to leave the classroom and fall to my knees in the lavatory until the spasm abated.

Eventually I was referred to a specialist—a former pupil—who laughed off my conviction that I was about to die and declared that I would dine on venison at his table at the end of two days. He brought me blessed relief without the intervention of surgery. I rattled the sharp-edged piece of coral in its glass container on the table at my hospital bedside; for me it sounded like heavenly music.

Fearing a recurrence of the agony, I consulted my surgeon friend on the advisability of spending a longer period in a colder part of the United States; in forthright fashion he said, "Chance it."

Hitherto I have confined my recollections to events in my small-town classroom, omitting other aspects of my life, especially those of the home, and my literary efforts. For the first time I now felt that these three lives were coalescing: as visiting lecturer at the famous International Creative Writing Program at the State University of Iowa I would be teaching in a way that so far I could only have conjured up in imagination. There a literary life would mate with a teaching life. The presence of my wife guaranteed a private home life.

Our family of five sons ("Bring forth men children only," I chanted as each one arrived)—Garry, Jim, Bryan, Maurice, and Owen—was all but reared. Three chose the law, influenced in no small way by their solicitor uncle in Tipperary, and another the civil service, and one wound up teaching, like his father. Financially it was difficult with two and at times three sons attending the university, but we managed, as many other parents did.

Kitty and I never experienced a moment's anxiety with these sons of ours. In the classroom they called me "sir"; outside the school gate they addressed me as "Dad." They were far more biddable and sensible than their father was as an adolescent. All now have wives of their own, with whom we are on the best of terms. I will spare my reader the ordeal of hearing me sing the praises of my seventeen grandchildren.

The famous Paul Engle, head of the International Creative Writing Program, I found as controlledly dynamic as his legend made me expect. I concluded that if one were in favour of his dream one could do no wrong; if one were lackadaisical about it one was in dire trouble at once.

I could identify with his aims. These were to make his course one of the most successful in the United States, evoking echoes throughout the world of literature, while I, God forgive me for the comparison, harboured the absurd notion of motivating a small town in Ireland, a speck on the map, to become a centre of the imagination in somewhat the same but much smaller way.

There was another parallel: Kerry and Iowa, like Newfoundland and Wigan, are the butt of professional jokers in their own countries. Such places tend to turn the tables on their mockers.

I faced my class. It was neither noisy nor mansion-housed. The International Creative Writing Program was for the most part then housed in temporary quarters while awaiting translation to a new building then under construction.

I was conscious of the traditions and record of the course. I had read a great deal about it at home in Ireland. Some of the lecturers were household names in America: Philip Roth had been there; Donald Judge, the poet, was on the staff. Flannery O'Connor from Georgia, a writer's writer if ever there was one, had as a student won an MFA from the course. ("Writing is a dusty trade. If you are afraid of having your hands soiled, do not bother with it. It's not a grand enough trade for you.") Perhaps she learnt the technicalities of the writing trade there; later she proved to be indomitably and uniquely herself in everything she wrote, and this despite the brevity of her life. She is one person I must try to visit before I leave this country, I told myself.

The students who faced me represented various national

groups. To gather them together in one college, Paul Engle had ranged widely, distance being no barrier in his search for talent. He had travelled not merely throughout North America and Europe but also further east, persuading governments, corporations and institutions to sponsor young students of literary promise so that they could participate. Talent is where you find it!

These were special students. They had to be taught the how of the short story and the what of its subject; but first the basic question: why does one write? For love, for money, for social effect, for freedom, for a new reality, for release from frustration, for participation in the mystery of creation, for jest, or for cancelling mortality—the list is endless.

How does one write? The short answer is *solvitur scribendo*—it is solved by the act of writing. The subject? The recognition of the seminal idea in a chance encounter is of vital importance. Then there is the gestation period deep in the imagination, with the labour pains of the mind indicating that the story is ready to be born.

I had developed and made my own a method derived from a comment made either by Seán Ó Faoláin or Frank O'Connor (I incline to Ó Faoláin, though neither of these great writers has mentioned this method in the book on the short story each has written). Meeting me by appointment in a tea-shop in Dublin, both had welcomed me to the pages of *The Bell*. Playing the part of the artless tiro up from Kerry, I asked, let us say Ó Faoláin, "How do you write a short story?" He smiled and replied enigmatically, "You get a male idea and a female idea. You couple them, and the children are short stories." This is a phrase that governed my entire writing life thereafter.

A local radio programme helped me to reach out beyond the

confines of my classroom in Iowa City. I was asked by the station to broadcast for half an hour twice a week. "What do I say?" I asked. "Doesn't really matter what you say: they're only listening to your accent."

I accepted the offer. I read some of my own stories, sang ballads, recited poetry, and talked about anything that came into my head. What I did not know at the time was that the tape of my talk was being copied and lent to several other radio stations. Soon I realised that I had a wide listening public in the mid-west.

I had many responses from what to me up to then was a white void of territory. It enabled me to make contact with an old friend, a pastor of a hill parish who came down to the city looking for me, which resulted, when the weather grew kinder, in a visit to his isolated presbytery and church high in the snow-silent hills. We talked the weekend away; at his insistence I had to begin at the outermost suburbs of our native town and name every citizen old and new, moving from door to door down the street. After a meal I'd begin on another street, giving a commentary as before. Then a repast, and off again with the cataract of nostalgic stories, the pair of us roaring with laughter at some almost forgotten incident or character dredged up from our shared boyhood.

It was in Iowa over an early breakfast that I read the headlines: "He is dead in Dublin, the rebel playwright and playboy who wrote and sang his way into the heart of his people." The picture of Brendan Behan with his broad features and semi-toothless smile behind a raised glass stared at me from the front page.

Later that day, as I walked back to my flat, I saw that the main bookshop of the city had cleared its front window. A photograph of Brendan stood on a silver tray; beside it was a half-drained glass of beer, with an empty bottle standing beside it. A half-smoked cigarette still held its long grey ash.

I stood looking at it for a long time. I saw the symbolism in the tribute, but the beer bottle conveyed a certain irony. Its label identified it as Bass. Perhaps alone in that city I recalled that a Colonel Gretton of the Bass brewing company had made a statement on Irish affairs that Brendan and his comrades deeply resented, so much so that for a time there was an attempted boycott of that particular brand of beer (prompting *Dublin Opinion* to record the "epitaph for a recalcitrant publican: *Fuair sé Bass.*")

"What's the difference between the real writer and the sham writer?" Brendan once asked me after he had pitched down his paint tin in the office of *The Bell* in Dublin. "The real writer," I replied, "is crazy and has a hell of a time pretending to be sane; the sham writer is sane and has a hell of a job pretending to be crazy." He used to shout this after me later whenever and wherever we met. "I'm still pretending to be sane," was always his parting cry.

The harmonisation of disparates, the reconciliation of opposites, was the prime proposition I wished to establish as the means of writing a short story. Since the unit of reference in a short story is generally the human being (it could also be a whale, a tiger, or a clock beetle) it is worth while considering this unit in the particular light of a story or tale.

With this in mind I regress to myself at the age of fourteen and recall the words of an old west Kerry fisherman who examined and compared the caught mackerel in the palm of his hand as the curach bobbed like a cork in the Blasket Sound.

"Isn't it extraordinary that the Almighty never created two mackerel in the ocean with the same pattern on their skins?" Sick as I was, I found myself compelled to pick up pair after pair of fish and verify what the man had just said. To my jaundiced eye and under the wan light of daybreak it seemed that what he said was true. The green and blue squiggles on the fish seemed to indicate that no two patterns tallied.

I looked up at the pearl-grey sky. It seemed incredible that not alone did each mackerel carry this mark of uniqueness but so did each human fingerprint, each blade of grass, each noseprint of a hound, each leaf, each superbly patterned snowflake seen under a microscope, each grain of sand, each insect. This uniqueness I saw as a kind of sanctity or holiness, which demanded respect in the case of each human being, whether mad, daft, abandoned, deformed—or embryonic. I suggested that it was this uniqueness, the existence of which obviously cannot be proved, given the variety of units involved, that a writer celebrates in his work.

Mention of God is highly unpopular in certain lecture halls of the United States. I had to present my theory as artfully and as circumspectly as I dared, while at the same time implying a certain scepticism on my part. "What do you think?" was the usual device used to avoid confrontation.

Having transferred some idea of the unique unit, I now went on to the coupling of opposites. I still carry in the recesses of my mind scores of uncoupled ideas in the form of situations, phrases, or faces, my overtures at mating them rejected time and again by my conscious or subconscious self. I asked myself if there was any way I could hasten the moment of mating—by a kind of artificial insemination as it were. I even went to the extremity of opening the dictionary at random, placing my fingertip haphazardly on words and then testing them in my mind for a possible fertilisation: an artistic marriage bureau, as it were, which I have on occasion found successful.

Each week or month in the writing class a student was expected to hand up a short story. I selected one of these—the writers of the other stories were counselled individually. Copies of the selected story were then given to each student (with the writer's name omitted), the story was studied for a few days, and then the class proceeded to criticise the effort.

At first I did not realise how severely this process could weigh upon the writer—who sometimes chipped in with a mild item of criticism simply to avoid identification! Little by little, by observing the drawn faces of the students, I realised what a hurtful process this could be. On one occasion, as a result of an incautious and slightly sarcastic contribution from myself, I saw the writer's face go deathly white. He did not turn up for several weeks; I had to seek him out and pacify him before he would return.

To make up for this lapse from prudence I thought of a plan. I had an unpublished story of my own, with a neutral background and subject matter, copied and issued in the usual way. I then called for the sternest treatment when assessing its worth. My own comments were uncompromising, even vituperative, at which the eyes of the students grew wider until at last the bravest among them led the critical hunt so as to be in at the final blooding.

There was complete silence as the class ended and I gathered my papers before leaving. The students looked at each other as if to learn from facial expressions which of them had been savaged. At the door I turned and said in a throwaway fashion, "You might like to know the identity of the writer of that particular story." I paused, and then said, "Myself"—and vanished. A roar of appreciative laughter pursued me.

At times, students were asked to write a paper on the literature of their particular area, country, or culture. This for me was immensely rewarding, and introduced me to layers of the literature of various countries.

One day, fearing that I had been placing undue emphasis on Ireland, I asked for a contribution of a completely different kind. A French-Canadian student made a little gesture of acceptance. "I'm glad," I said, "to have a contribution from French Canada, and from someone with no connection whatsoever with Ireland."

After the Easter break this young man handed in his paper, which he read and I praised. He asked to see me after class. He reminded me that before the break I had said that one could learn a great deal by looking at one's grandmother: "like seeing yourself in a mirror"; and that I had said he hadn't a drop of Irish blood in his veins. "I looked up my grandma in Upper Canada—only saw her once before. Her name before she married was Kitty MacMahon. Her father was Bryan MacMahon from the County Kerry."

Having experienced the high summer of Boston and Cambridge, I was thankful to sample the cold rural sections of the United States on weekends, particularly in areas of Irish settlement. Some had pushed westwards from the east coast on wagons drawn by oxen, while others came on foot. Reading the names on the roadside mail-boxes we often found a succession of *Macs*, *Os*, and *Murphys*, followed by sections of German or Scandinavian surnames.

Homesteads in the mid-west can be half a mile apart, so the

visit of one born in Ireland can be an experience for both parties. The Irish-Americans' concept of Ireland and scraps of ancestral lore, often naïve in the extreme, can be endearing. University students from such sections, and of all national groups, have a limited experience of the range of personalities to whom one is exposed in the Irish small town, village, or countryside—"a standing army of colourful extras," as a critic commented in a review of a short story collection of mine. This paucity of experience can be reflected in the portrayal of fictional characters in the mid-west.

With significant exceptions, fiction writing in the United States is confined to the university scene. When exposed fully to the variety of the Irish experience here in Ireland, the sensitive American student tends to blossom.

In the lecture room I laboured on with the short story. I was unsure of what I could stimulate into life. The first sentence is the "Open, Sesame" to the cave of wonders. It should convey information, and tempt one to read on. Time, place, position, angle of light, purpose, viewpoint, person or character, a clear problem, dialogue, pace, and the cryptic use of obliqueness to appeal to the senses of the reader—all these must be borne in mind. Adjectives and adverbs are barnacles slowing up the progress of the racing boat of the story. Concrete words, Anglo-Saxon for the most part; vital transitive verbs; identification with character; short sentences for mounting tension; first suggested solution to posed problem, second ditto, final resolution, which may even be an invitation to the reader to supply his own—all these are parts of the hypnosis exercised by the writer and in which the foregoing factors or rules are fused and used intuitively. And balance above all else! This only indicates the craft—the lust for telling must be supplied by nature.

There are many other technical subtleties to be employed or conveyed in the small space allowed the short-story writer. He would do well to remember that the short story is a telegram with a charge on each word.

Kitty and I flew down to Atlanta early in Easter week to visit dear friends of ours, Dick and Clare Dodd of Marshallville, Georgia. Dick and I have been writing to each other for well over forty years; few people know me better. I had been looking forward to this visit for a long time, and our reunion was a joyous one. The weather in the south was warm, and the red earth reminded me of the clay in the Dingle Peninsula seen after a shower of rain. The South of story, stage and film came alive, with all its props and personalities: old black folk with crops of snow-white hair sitting on the stoops of see-through cabins (the young had gone north to Washington or other northern cities), a few final cotton bolls wagging their heads in the breeze and the flashing succession of shingles telling of various religious sects were just as I had already experienced them in my imagination, so that I had a sense of being part of the place.

"Do we pass close to Milledgeville?" I asked Dick as we drove southwards. "Yes," he said. "I have a letter of introduction to Flannery O'Connor," I told him. "No problem." We drove through Milledgeville and out into the countryside to the O'Connor farmstead. In my mind's eye I had pictured this farm several times before. The red clay, the luxuriant shrubbery, the mounting heat, the grating cry of the peacocks—a sound I had always associated with the brilliant but stricken writer whom I had looked forward to meeting—all coalesced in my mind to yield a mood of full awareness.

A pair of black servants, the man with his hands concealed

in the sleeves of his cardigan, the woman complementing his courtesy, materialised from some shrubbery to say, "Miss Flannery knows you are to come, but she is seriously ill and under sedation." Awake, she would be glad to chat to us. She was looking forward to our visit. So near, so far!

I scribbled a note; as I finished it I made an awkward gesture to my friend Dick, and my inscribed presentation pen flashed through the air and fell into dense shrubbery. And there, I presume, it remains. Re-entering the car I found myself inconsequentially parodying the title of one of Flannery O'Connor's books, *A Good Pen is Hard to Find*.

Behold me later that day swaying gently back and forth on the rocking-chair on Dick Dodd's porch. His is a beautiful antebellum mansion set in the magnolia-scented depths of Georgia. Dick can read me like a book; I suffer from the delusion that I can read him. His passions are for hunting-dogs (on harness after game birds, with the huntsman on horseback), horses, and good literature. In a letter to me many years ago old Séamus MacManus had described him as the most interesting and vital man he had met in a lifetime of lecturing in every part of the United States.

We felt at home in Marshallville; when I visited America later this noble house proved to be a haven of rest, where I relaxed much as a salmon rests behind a rock on its turbulent journey upstream in the spring. Dick's wife, Clare, née O'Brien— a niece of the novelist Kate O'Brien, the pride of literary Limerick, and of Ireland for that matter—made us truly welcome. It was an area of peaches, pecan nuts, and camellias. Not on a commercial basis but for the love of these blossoms Dick cultivated camellias under the trees in the extensive woods and nurseries, which his uncle had bestowed on the Camellia Society of the United States. Two new varieties he named "Bryan MacMahon" and "Kitty MacMahon" in his colourful personal catalogues. Other varieties he named for some old fishing friends in Ireland.

Dick and I talked of literature, of course—not indeed as a school subject, for Dick is a close reader who can pierce the counterfeit to the core. Naturally we spoke of Faulkner, Ransom, Davidson, Warren, and Welty, but we always wound up talking at length on Ireland. At the time of my first visit to Georgia both Dick's parents were living in a bungalow close by. I struck up a brief but cordial relationship with the older Mrs Dodd. I cannot readily forget the smiling way this gracious woman looked into my eyes and said, "Ah, Ireland! We had great difficulty weaning Dick off Ireland."

Back at base in Iowa City to gather up the loose ends and allocate grades to the students in preparation for returning to Ireland, I received a phone call as I left the radio studio.

"Last year I went to Ireland specially to visit you, and missed you. I'm a priest, Father John Peters by name, pastor of an old Irish settlement on the Mississippi to the north of Iowa City." He added, "I'm driving down to Iowa City on Friday to bring you back up here for the weekend." He came. He saw. Kitty and I were conquered. The visit to Harper's Ferry (there is a more historic Harper's Ferry in American history) gave me first-hand experience of an Irish settlement over a hundred years old set down in a countryside of bold contours, with the mighty Mississippi exercising a profound influence on its daily life.

A surprise awaited us. In the spacious church hall, the whole parish had assembled to see a real Irishman and hear him speak. I spoke on Ireland and its dire history of emigration. I told how it was coping with the many pressures of a nation old in years but young in the experience of self-government. Later I asked for questions.

Shy to start, after a while those present responded freely. They enquired about the Irish villages their forebears had long since left. The survival of family surnames in the old areas intrigued them. Towards the end of my talk a very old man stood up; in a voice quavering with age and emotion he said, "When I was a child my grandfather, then a very old man who had left Ireland as a child, always said his prayers in Irish. Please let me hear again what the prayers sound like."

There was no sound in the basement hall as slowly I made the Comhartha na Croise and recited in turn the Ár nAthair, Is É Do Bheatha, and Glóire. It was all I could do to finish the prayers when I saw the tears flowing down over a cheek here and there among my congregation.

From headstone to headstone I walked through the wide cemetery beside the church, reading the names of the Irish dead. On some of the stones the counties of their births were spelt phonetically—County Meade, County Galloway—bringing the vision of the early settlers vividly to mind. The final surprise came on examining a Celtic cross standing apart at the edge of the cemetery at a point that offered a wide view of the land and riverscape. I read the inscription on it with a mounting sadness. It was the grave of a Father John Costello from Castleisland, a member of a family well known to me. "Well, well," I said, "is it here you lie, Father John, far from the fields around your beloved Island of Kerry."

At an Irish-American seminar held later elsewhere in the United States I spoke of these settlements. What struck me forcefully about these areas was how Irish customs still obtained, despite a considerable sea-change. On Saturday evenings at Confession time I observed in the church the men kneeling on one knee ("ecclesiastical fowlers taking aim at Almighty God" was how our indignant curate at home described them), the peak of their flat cloth caps covering their mouths as they awaited the opportunity to dart into an empty confession box. This practice was typical of the Ireland of my boyhood; watching the penitents I realised then that I could well have been in an Irish village of sixty years before, in Duagh in Kerry, Tulla in Clare, or Boherlahan in Tipperary. It came as no surprise to me to be told that at the wakes held some years before my arrival the exact rubrics of an Irish rural wake were observed.

My one regret is that I never got the opportunity to visit Peterborough, deep in Ontario, a city with a population then of sixty thousand. The city had its beginnings in the Peter Robinson immigration settlement of 1825 with 2,024 people, mostly from south-western Ireland. Villages with names such as Ennismore (a Listowel townland) and Emily have surnames found in the roll of any rural Irish school and that stir the heartstrings with memories of that first leaving of Ireland. The story of that migration, largely unknown and unappreciated here at home, deserves a better fate than that of Irish negligence. These kinsfolk of ours, carefully selected from sixty thousand applicants, set out in search of a new world and a new life. Their goal was a promised land where their descendants could attain to the fullness and goodness of living, something denied them in Ireland.

Clare Galvin from the Peterborough area, author of *The Holy Land*, often visits Ireland and his far-out kinsfolk in my home area; doing so he bridges a gap of 167 years with the original founders of a community that each year sends a representative to the Rose of Tralee Festival. I never see his calm, aristocratic features without thinking back to his ancestor, young Paddy Galvin of Rathea, a townland in the hills above Listowel. After an epic journey by land and sea, as the crowded scow crossing Chemona Lake approached the site of the first settlement, Paddy leaped from the craft and, wading ashore, turned and shouted to the others, "Tell your children and your children's children that I, Paddy Galvin, was the first person to set foot on the Holy Land." My formal reception of Clare Galvin before a gathering of his surviving distant cousins in Listowel was some compensation for my failure to visit our distant townfolk.

Not much more to do except to wrap up in Iowa, say our goodbyes to Paul Engle and others, and set out for home, sightseeing en route along the shores of Lake Michigan with Father Peters at the wheel.

One incident on that journey remains fixed in my mind. "You Irish?" asked the man at the lunch counter where we stopped for coffee. "My old pastor, who is just now dying on his feet, would sure appreciate a final visit from Irish folk." He pointed to a presbytery some two hundred yards away down a side road; we consented—how could we refuse?

When we were shown into the drawing-room we found ourselves surrounded by representations of horses. Paintings, charcoal drawings, statuettes of black and white horses were everywhere. Presently, led by the man we met, now revealed as a curate, the old pastor, wearing a black dressing-gown, came tottering down the stairs, step after faltering step. He greeted us graciously but feebly. His assistant signed to us to do most of the talking.

We talked of Ireland. The old pastor said little but listened attentively, nodding his head at intervals. Tottering back slowly to the stairway he mounted painfully some steps when, with difficulty, he turned and raised his trembling hand—for attention or in blessing, we could not tell which. In a clear but quavering voice he said, "Give my love to Roscommon and to the horses of Roscommon."

The ship's whistle sounded. We felt the deck throbbing faintly under our shoes. From the rail we gave a final wave to Father Peters far below. The vessel began to move away from the tall walls of Manhattan.

As, at last, the immense buildings faded into mist, I found myself delivering a final (or semi-final?) verdict on the United States: a good country to go to, and a good country to come home from.

CHAPTER THIRTEEN

No matter how high a bird will fly
It has to come down for water.

I had to come back to earth—not unwillingly, let it be said—and return to the country-town school and put aside (for the present?) my transatlantic experience. It was now 1965; my year of retirement on age grounds would be 1975. I had a clear decade to run, God willing, and if I stayed full-time in teaching service.

That "if" is important. I had already had overtures to take up a full-time or part-time lecturing post in the American university circuit. One offer was tempting. I mulled over it, not really wishing to succumb. Why these invitations? I asked myself.

I concluded that in the case of faculties that place the accent on creative literature, while they could procure lecturers who could write but not teach and others who could teach but not write, it was difficult to find someone who could both teach and write.

The temptation continued to nag me. In three years in America I could earn as much as I could in the decade of active teaching years remaining to me at home, where the payment of surtax—because of literary royalties—stuck in my craw. Furthermore, the sum of my actual teaching days in America would be little more than six months in the year; the remaining six months could find me back in Ireland and having the best of both worlds. There was also the prospect of a new, exciting life opening up for me in America, where the writer is accorded a high status.

But what would I do without the Irish dimension to life—without the cut and thrust of banter, the laughter and the ballads, the summer playground of the west coast, the observance of the interplay and counterplay of local politics and intrigue, the mart-day meetings with country people, the in-for-a-chat of old friends and neighbours, the delightful discussion of books with my friend the retired librarian, the evening walks with Ned—all the minutiae of small-town living placed on the pan to balance that of material gain and superficial recognition?

So, even when lifelong friends in America offered me delightful places to live and write in I would equivocate, saying, "I'm very grateful. Please let me think this out." Still the tempter continued to whisper. "You are failing to meet the challenge. You are turning your back on a wider world. In America, for the first time, your vocation and avocation will be conjoined. You will not be pulled two ways, as you now are."

More important consideration still: how would Kitty take the transition? Essentially she was a homemaker who did not relish public appearances and had always tried to avoid having her photograph taken. Flowers, furniture, delph and family were her world. The first primrose of the year could afford her transports of joy. She was completely at home with the staff wives in America—but she knew exactly when she was returning to Ireland.

This was a happy period in my school life. We had good conditions in the new building. The inspection system had become humane, the managerial system equally so. Outside school life I wrote close to the moral bone in various ways; but now, for the first time in my small-town life, there was the understanding that the writer was an explainer and explorer of outback regions in human behaviour and so allowed the reader to vicariously examine and codify certain murkier aspects of the self.

Not all my reminiscences are happy. The word "eucalyptus" triggers sadness in my mind.

Now that I'm out for quite a while on fertile grass in the twilight of retirement, I often pass the school building in the half-darkness of evenings. When there is no-one about I cross over the stile and see how the eucalyptus trees are coming along— these were planted by Paddy, a former pupil of mine, long after I had retired.

I roll a eucalyptus leaf between my palms, then bring my cupped hands to my nose and inhale deeply. At the same time I find myself looking into the play-shed in the school yard. The aromatic smell and the long play-shed coalesce in my mind to bring back a memory of my lifelong friend Ned Sheehy.

Almost every night for over fifty years Ned and I walked and talked in the streets or the Square of our town. When it rained we exercised in the school play-shed. Sometimes we discovered lovers seated in the darkest corner of the place. We stopped short of them: by unspoken pact we never greeted them, nor they us.

Ned had cars for hire—taxis, as they are called in the city. He was in touch with many activities in south-west Ireland. Hurling and football matches, weddings, christenings, funerals, midnight illnesses, political crises, returned exiles, family celebrations— every day provided Ned or one of his drivers with unforeseen excitements. He never broke customer confidences, but came round the telling of a story in anonymous terms as if it had happened "up the country." A keen and tolerant student of human nature, he always compared a taxi to a confession box, with similar rules of secrecy.

"Night after night walking around—what do the pair of you get to talk about?" an old woman would ask us. I couldn't explain. What lay beyond the grave was a common topic. The value of education too—Ned saw that his children got the best.

By instinct I could tell to the second when he had left his house; I would walk half way across the town to meet him. One rainy night as we paraded in our dark shelter I found Ned unusually silent.

"What's wrong?" I asked at last.

He paused, then, turning his face to the wall, "I won't be with you long more," he said.

"Why?"

"Got my walking papers today."

"What do you mean?"

"Results of a biopsy," he said. "I've got the Big C."

I was thunderstruck. I paused. "Hell, Ned," I said, "you'll beat that rap."

"I've got six weeks."

Then, "Have you told them at home?" from me.

"No; I'll tell them when I have to. Please don't mention it."

Ned and I were together in Mogan, a little village up the coast from Puerto Rico in the Canaries. I was writing some slogans in Irish to be placed in the window of a nearby restaurant.

We were laughing at nothing at all. I was seated under a eucalyptus tree. A leaf drifted down to my knees. I caught it and rubbed it between my palms. "Smell," I said to Ned. "I never knew that before," he said as he smelled the fragrant oil.

North of Los Gigantes in Tenerife there is a town called Garachico at the foot of a mighty mountain cliff over which a road zigzags perilously to the main roadway far above. A superb driver, Ned loved to "gun" a little SEAT car against the terrifying angle of this cliffside. Doing so he would give a fairground shout of "Once again, daring James Marshall takes the Wall of Death!" My heart was in my mouth until we reached the top. Ned took the real Wall of Death in a similar fashion. He died bravely and calmly.

If I thought I was finished with America, America was not finished with me. Lawrence, picturesque Lawrence, with its constituent college of Kansas University, I recall with pride—and sorrow.

It concerns approximately a hundred American students who spent some months in Inishbofin off the Galway coast. The frontier spirit is still vibrant in the American mid-west; and when dedicated and idealistic professors called to my door asking for advice in this regard I gave it to the best of my ability. To sample the real Ireland was their goal: they had already sampled Greece and Rome, and lecturing their students in situ had produced a splendid reaction. Beginning in February they arranged to spend five months on Inishbofin, a place I knew well.

They sent me word asking me to meet the group in Shannon on a certain date and to travel with them to the island. Another engagement prevented me from doing so. Picture my shock and sorrow on hearing on the radio some days later that two young members of the group had been drowned on the island. They had climbed a tall crag at a place on the coast called the Stags. After loitering for a while, on looking down they discovered to their horror that the rock was surrounded by the rising tide. Possibly unaware that they could have waited in safety until the tide had receded, the two young men jumped into the water, and were drowned.

I wrote a ballad on the Inishbofin drownings. It was a small tribute to academic idealism. Later a memorial window was dedicated to the students in the little island church. On a subsequent visit to the university at Lawrence to deliver a lecture, I was requested in the middle of the event to sing the ballad to an audience of students, staff members and above all the parents of the drowned boys. It was a most emotional experience.

Rummage among your youthful experience, I found myself whispering at times, the advice I had given in later American literary lectures. Search every inch of the place where you were born. Isolate the characters in your mind. The impressions gained in youth and adolescence are sharp-edged. Mull over these, and maybe a simple incident will indicate a common factor of human behaviour everywhere.

"I come from a small country town in south-west Ireland. I'm a local schoolteacher. The place is only a speck on the map. We cherish our characters, our heroes, our people of significance. Would you care to hear about them?"

I talked about "our town" much as Thornton Wilder or Dylan Thomas might have done. I told them of the town crier who made his announcements in crude verse, of neighbour Kathy who went off to become head cook in the White House, serving three presidents, and who, as I heard her tell my mother, could tell that a crisis had loomed in US politics when the sandwiches came down from upstairs uneaten. I told of film star Mary Pickford, once the world's sweetheart, whose forebears, the Hennessys, were born within two hundred yards of my home; of the shopkeeper who kept the clippings of his fingernails in his sweaty hat-band and who took them down and chewed them when perplexed; of the odd old fellow who didn't trust banks to guard his savings and whose last chore each night was to totter to the town square, where he bumped the bank door with his buttocks to make sure it was securely locked; of the man who could not become accustomed to the new bathroom his wife had insisted on installing and who took to the lanes and fields to relieve himself; of the venerable neighbour who had driven a Wells Cargo stage coach in Missouri and who knew the James boys, who, it is believed, came of north Kerry stock; and of many others. If I pretended to forget my stint of gossip at the close of a lecture, I was quickly reminded of it.

In the course of a lecture we often discussed the question of self-promotion by the writer. The word "gimmickry" was used. Should the writer call attention to himself to sell his wares? Can the aesthetic standards of critics be relied upon? Have newspapers a conscience? Are the theatrical antics of a writer an indication of the value of his work? Is the only bad publicity a writer experiences that of the obituary notice?

I must have overpraised the Irish way of life, as over the years many American students of mine turned up in Kerry, saying, "It's just as you said, and much more!"

On the rundown in an active life inside and outside school, I have often tried to isolate what it was that kept me going. There were dark periods, of course; each late November the black dog padded behind me, only to be shooed away by the comradeship abroad at Christmastide. But in the dark times, like the man with whom I drank coffee recently and who quoted for me a beautiful passage on friendship, I too fall back on the same author, Emerson, and chanted half aloud and half in secret:

> Accept the place the Divine Providence has found for you, the society of your contemporaries, the connection of events. Great men have always done so, and confided themselves childlike to the genius of their age, betraying their perception that the absolutely trustworthy was seated at their heart, working through their hands, predominating in all their being. And we are now men, and must accept in the highest mind, the same transcendent destiny, and not minors and invalids in a protected corner, not cowards fleeing before a revolution, but guides, redeemers and benefactors, obeying the Almighty effort and advancing on chaos and the dark.

The chanting of that quotation has always recharged my batteries. Again and again I have had recourse to the quotation from *The Crock of Gold* by James Stephens already mentioned, which continued to console and absolve me whenever I lapsed from grace. Probing it more fully, I found its implication clear: man is an amalgam of the divine and the feral. To reckon man as a godhead is ludicrous, as being wholly bestial equally so. In effect he is a reconciliation of opposites. If he ever denies the brute in his nature and arrogantly claims that he is superhuman—therein lie the seeds of complete dissolution.

Remorselessly the years of the teaching decade remaining to me peeled off one by one. My life was still a full one. We had a pleasant staff and few or no disciplinary problems. Outside the school, life was equally satisfactory. My sons had qualified and were getting married. "Settling down" is the term used; the phrase always reminds me of a dog turning round and round in long grass before lying down.

I was having success with my stories in various parts of the world. I flew to Germany to see a translation of my novel come off the press. I translated *Peig,* the autobiography of that noble islander, into English. A pageant of mine continued to run in the castle of Knappogue in Clare; eventually over sixteen years it was seen by half a million people. I did all kinds of literary work, rarely turning down an invitation.

I spoke at many public functions. I had a considerable daily post to occupy my attention, and I tried to answer every letter I received. I was overwhelmed with manuscripts. My "honest opinion" was all the correspondent asked; sometimes when I gave it it was received in dour silence. Ah, well, such is life.

I continued to read assiduously, and never let a day pass without having completed a writing stint. My seat at the harnessmaker's was reserved for me. I indulged my passion for islands. I was up to my neck in the tricky world of drama.

My old friend Liam, classical scholar and master of the Irish language, retired some years before me. He had been principal teacher of a country school some miles outside the town. His letter of description of his retirement day was, as became him, in Latin. In truth, I saw Liam as the last real scholar of the court of Ciceronian Latin recorded in the Kerry of a century ago.

To offer a sampling of the hinterland and its respect for the classical forms of life and letters, I refer to "Sir Bob." As town schoolmaster and old friend it was my weekly duty to solemnly give him a mildly Rabelaisian subject on which to make a sonnet. Armed with his subject he would return home and compose a sonnet to be handed up to me on the Saturday following.

He had a felicitous if earthen turn of phrase; the subjects I offered him were in harmony with his innocent but talented turn of mind. He composed "Sonnet on a Cow Dung," "Sonnet on a Load of Hay," "Sonnet on King Puck," and many more. The one I remember best was his "Sonnet to a Chamberpot." He was delighted when I gave him this subject. He went home, took out the utensil, placed it on a chair, and, with his tongue in his cheek and in a spirit of impish delight, began to compose. His extremely tolerant wife murmured, "I see you have visited the master."

Gifted personalities like "Sir Bob" are prized far beyond the bounds of kinship. The whole community takes pride in such personalities and regards them as its own. Alas, nowadays they are replaced by soap opera on television.

Psychosomatic—that's the word I'm looking for: a disease caused or aggravated by mental strain or stress.

With me it began a year or so before retirement day, which for a teacher is regarded as the thirtieth of June following his sixty-fifth birthday. That year I look back upon with a sensation akin to that of fever.

I found myself at the mercy of a single nagging force, like a rat gnawing at my vitals. At times I trembled at the knees—a weakness I had only previously experienced on the occasion of beginning an impromptu public address. With some measure of identification I thought of the ballad entitled "The Rocks of Bawn" and the plight of the unfortunate labouring man who complained,

> *My legs are always tremb-al-in'*
> *For fear I might give in.*

So it was with me. Some faint voice deep in my consciousness seemed continually to be asking, "When you retire, what are you going to do? How are you going to exist without the harsh but delightful rhythm of the school day? How are you going to occupy your active mind? Are you going to end your days as the small-town bore, living in the past and exhausting everyone with idiotic anecdotes? Are you going to shave only when your face is stubble-littered? Abandon collar and tie? (What a relief that would be!) Is it possible to begin a new life when you lock the school door behind you for the last time?

In class I was short-tempered, given to flaring up on small pretexts. The children seemed unspeakably stupid. "You're the worst class I've ever taught," I told them. They looked up at me with a kind of baffled yet understanding stare. On occasion I found myself shouting. Self-righteous, I seemed faced with a conspiracy of non-cooperation. I would not stand for it!

A cold penetrated the marrow of my bones, superimposed on the psychosomatic shiver, and I found myself moaning in hospital. Despite exhaustive tests the doctors could find nothing wrong. "Subclinical virus" was what they finally came up with. I had my own ideas. Pre-retirement brethren, be warned; but not alarmed.

One quiet boy seemed to fully understand my problem. He faced me calmly and fearlessly. At most he was nine years of age. At the height of my ill temper he answered my defiant question with composed assurance. His gentle eyes were tolerant. Belatedly, I thank him: he saved me a great deal of anguish.

I sought a cure for my ailment: I would renew my lifelong resolution. Again I found myself standing before the map of Europe. I would walk the Pyrenees in easy stages, the foothills from west to east. There was Stevenson's book *Travels with a*

Donkey in the Cevennes—I would re-read that first. Unlike Sean-Phádraic Ó Conaire, I would do without the ass. That was it! With a pack on my back and walking-shoes, I'd make the journey of a lifetime.

This resolve buoyed me up for a while. If I never achieved it, what harm was done—a man is nothing without a mental hideaway. April or September, I concluded, would be the best time to undertake this therapeutic expedition.

I did something else by way of immediate therapy. At night the dark, empty school assumed a different character, its classrooms not noisy now but each one more like a confession box, where at one and the same time one could be both confessor and penitent. I would go to the school at midnight, sit there in the silent classroom, and, conscious of the bulk of the hill seen vaguely against the southern skyline through the wide classroom window, I would review the changes I had seen during my lifetime from this small academic perch in the cage of a country town.

No sooner resolved than executed; that very midnight found me seated in the now mysterious box of reflection. What changes have you seen in your time—changes not only educational but social, cultural, economic, or whatever? Higgledy-piggledy, let the thoughts come!

I've seen the periwinkle and the pin replaced by the prawn cocktail and the cocktail stick. I've seen the cottage card game of forty-five replaced by the poker classic, with prizes of a thousand pounds, and the turkey raffle yield place to a national lottery with weekly rewards of over a million pounds. I've seen an end to the white coffin borne to the cemetery by poorly dressed ex-soldiers holding white ribbons. I've seen children's lunches change dramatically—a bottle of milk and the purple school cocoa replaced by Mars bars, packets of biscuits or crisps, and lemonade in tins. (I failed dismally to keep the school playground free of litter.)

Annual outings to the seaside on the quaintest railway in the world are replaced by holidays in Las Americas or Mykinos. I've seen the breakfast of porridge replaced with a pettish choice of ten different cereals; plebeian bacon and cabbage have given way to lasagne verde and quiche Lorraine. I've heard the "Hello" of greeting supplanted by a transatlantic "Hi." The price of a garden spade I've seen increase fiftyfold and more (ah for the memory of Eoghan Rua Ó Súilleabháin, that adorable scamp who fashioned a superb poem out of his asking a blacksmith to make just such a spade!); I've grown dismal at the clichés of newspaper headings like "tug of love" and snapshots (a good old word that!) of majorettes from Chattanooga doing a soft-shoe shuffle at the St Patrick's Day Parade in Ballynabucht.

I've seen the rise and fall of Kepler's Malt, Harrison's Pomade, Zambuk, Monkey Brand (won't wash clothes), Van Houten's Cocoa, and Magic Spot Balls.

One thatched house is left in a town where in my boyhood there were hundreds. There is not a trace of the shawls that once indicated social rank—black, biscuit-coloured Paisley, chocolate-brown, and green-and-black plaid. Good riddance, perhaps—all were full of fleas. I've seen the celluloid world of Tom Mix and Mary Pickford yield to the lipsticked world of Joan Collins et al. The outlawed ballad has now become a select vestry psalm; I took a hand in its enthronement. Now I stand by and watch as gradually it becomes flyblown. I've seen an empire disintegrate before my eyes and note how its unnatural boundaries leave savage civil wars in its wake. I've seen the fire on the hearthstone replaced by the microwave cooker.

For the first eleven years of my life Ireland was part of the British Empire, with all the indignities that connoted. I then experienced the first fever of liberty; I ncw dread the new imperialism of materialism, its prime weapon manipulation. In my bones and brain I am convinced that nothing happens naturally any more, that everything and everyone is engineered by schemers and conditioned by image, projection, package, and presentation.

There is a sound from outside. I open the classroom door and enter the cloakroom. There the windows begin at shoulder level. There is a smell of damp tweed from three or four abandoned overcoats. I tiptoe to the window. Just outside and crouched among the little garden plots is the figure of a youngish man. He is barely four or five feet from me. Bending over the school plots, he is filling the pockets of his old trench coat with brussels sprouts. As he stands up and moves sidelong to pack his pockets with onions, radishes, and lettuce, I turn away from the window. I do not wish to recognise him.

Why should I? Reprimand is the loose change of the overlord. Whoever he is, this man is my neighbour. He will enjoy the fresh garden fare. But me no buts. I will not rob him of his dignity. What? Confront him and make an enemy in my own community? You must be mad. I recall the boyhood raids I made with friends on orchards within five miles of town. Peaches from glasshouses, too—who am I to throw stones?

How to warn him without giving open insult? I retreat to the cloakroom door, find the switch, and flash the light on and off just once. I wait. Through the classroom window I vaguely see him stomp across the dark playing-field. His raincoat is pulled up about his ears. Is he mystified? So brief was the light that he may have thought it a lightning flash.

It's all part of life. Especially of small-town life.

About this time I received an honorary doctorate of laws from the National University, "for services to literature." I like to recall that my teaching years were mentioned on the citation read by my proposer, Professor Tadhg Carey, then president of University College, Cork, as a recognition of the work of very many national teachers throughout Ireland.

There I was, all dressed up, listening to my praises being sung and about to approach President Éamon de Valera, acting in his capacity as chancellor of the university. Greeting me, he bent forward and, with a twinkle in his eye and a sidelong glance at Dr Séamus Wilmot, the registrar—the first man to encourage me to write—whispered, "Lios Tuathail abú!"—Up Listowel! My sons, ranged around, were not so unctuous: one said to another, "Wouldn't that be the right gear in which to lay out the oul' fella?" When I heard the comment I countered with, "There you are. Never attended university and I finish up with a doctorate." This was met with, "Dad, look how long it took you to graduate." Too late I recalled Paddy Kavanagh's lines:

> I have a feeling
> That through the hole in reason's ceiling
> I can win to knowledge
> Without ever going to college.

However, I let them have the last word. They were coming; I was going.

Was this a time for levity, or for celebration? Both, I reckon. At times in life I have been jocose and evasive, even sarcastic.

Probably it's the mask I wear to cover the uncertainty, even the fear of the unknown.

Dies irae. The day of ire—or delight—for a retiring teacher is the last day of the school year. The summer holidays began about that time, so I reckoned I could blunt the edge of severance by telling myself that I would be back in the classroom again on the first of September or thereabouts.

Here and there throughout the country other teachers would be retiring on that day. I wondered how many of those who had been trained with me were leaving on the same date as I was. Very few, I told myself, had taught full-time.

My leavetaking, unlike that described by John McGahern in his novel on the subject, was pleasant. Unknown to me, the other teachers or parents—one parent in particular—had alerted RTE, so that when I opened the school door the children who trooped in after me were polished, as the saying goes, "to the veins of nicety." The other teachers tackled the end-of-year rolls with zest, and the salary forms were completed and signed so that that chore was off my shoulders. My book list for the following school year had also been circulated, so I did not find the morning passing.

Refreshments were smuggled in, not all of them non-alcoholic. Sandwiches made their appearance, also cakes and confectionery. The children had surreptitious little parcels under the desks, which I was not supposed to notice. One by one they left their places and quietly placed a gift on the table.

Secretly I had learnt to my keen delight that the staffs had decided to present me with a large copper plaque—the work of Tony, a staff member and a brilliant worker in copper—representing scenes from my play and novel *The Honey Spike*.

This remains one of my most precious possessions.

I was due to go home for lunch. As I went down the corridor a large-eyed infant took his sandwich from his mouth and looked up at me. "Mr MacMahon," he chirped. "I know why you won't be here any more." "Why?" I asked. "Because you're old and you're going to die." "The very reason," I said. "You're a clever child." I felt in good humour at once.

At the street corner an elderly man I had taught as a boy spoke up. "Your last day?" he enquired. "That's right," I said. "Watch yourself now, master," he said; "fellas like you finish up funny."

A genteel old woman paused as she passed me by. "Was it all boys you taught up there in the school?" "Yes," I said. "No girls?" "None." "Ach, sure you're only half a schoolmaster," came her verdict on my lifetime of endeavour.

Returning to school, I found a television crew in possession of my classroom. As they filed in, the children suddenly grew quiet. "Don't look at the camera," I said as the lights came down upon us and the shots were taken, just as they were taken in the school for the opening night of Irish television. Pupils and parents were now to be joined by the television crew in the assembly hall. There was a knock at my room door; I was asked to release the children and wait in my room to be called.

For the last time I addressed the children with the orders I had used during the whole of my school life. "Go réidh," I said as they gathered up their books. Then "Seasaigí," "Iompaígí," "Siúlaigí." They marched out. The lad who closed the door—I still remember his eyes. I was alone.

I looked out through the sunlit slats of the blinds. There was the hill that over the years I had watched in all its moods and tenses. The copper beech in the old fort for which the town is named was in the full glory of its foliage. When I drew on the cords to flick out the sunlight shafting through the venetian blinds the classroom was filled with a greenish subaqueous light. Seated behind the desk on the little dais beneath the schoolroom maps I found myself once again in "the room of reflection."

Pushing aside the assortment of gifts, I began to doodle on the blank page of a copybook before me. I found myself listing the names of the teachers with whom I had served in both adjoining schools over the years.

> *Michael senior; Joanna, Jerry, Jim,*
> *Frank and Mai, Maureen and Tim,*
> *Mícheál, Peg, Martin, and PJ,*
> *With Cathal, John and Joan I passed my day.*
> *There's Ellen, Tony, Eleanor, and Pidge—*
> *Across the years I build a reminiscent bridge,*
> *With Seán and Liam, Roddy, Mike, and Dick.*
> *And ere, in doggerel, I turn the final trick,*
> *Memory brings Benny and Liscarroll Ned,*
> *Some still alive; the most, alas, are dead.*

This caper finished and my poetic genius having petered out, I looked over the empty benches of the classroom. As I did so two images presented themselves to me. The first concerned the story told of an old schoolmaster who once taught and lived in my own barony. After his retirement he lived long into the dotage of his middle nineties. The window of the bedroom in which he lay semi-inert for several years opened onto a meadow. One summer day, men, women and children alike saving the hay outside stopped work on hearing the old teacher's raised voice issuing from the window. Clustering about the casement they heard the old man vibrantly calling the roll of children who had attended the nearby school seventy years before. Some of the names called were those of grandparents and great-grandparents of the haymakers. As the roll-call ended his head fell to one side and the old teacher died.

My second image had to do with a semi-autobiographical play of mine called *The Master*. In the penultimate scene I had foreshadowed the moment of retirement. I had inserted into the play a scene reminiscent of the ending of a classical story by Alphonse Daudet entitled *The Last Lesson*. This scene shows the interior of a village school on the Franco-Prussian border where, as the Prussian army marched in to occupy the area, the schoolmaster teaches the last lesson to be taught in French in the village. The villagers, young and old, crowd into the classroom; to the accompaniment of the increasing crunch of German boots on the roadway outside, the lesson ends. Then the old schoolmaster, his voice breaking with emotion, turns and, taking up a stick of chalk, writes on the blackboard the words *Vive la France!*

For me both images coalesced. As I looked over the empty benches of the classroom I murmured the roll-call of the living and the dead, and as I did so, a jostle of faces confronted me.

Some of those who answered me did so from the ends of the earth. Many of them lay beneath the earth. Those who answered indicated all manners of trades and professions. There were priests, teachers, lawyers, jockeys, horse and hound trainers, bankers, balladmakers like Seán, a biographer called Anthony, an actor named Éamon, and a playwright named John. Pilots of planes, millionaires and bums, air company executives, tinkers and tailors, soldiers and civil servants, together with a well-loved Down's Syndrome child or two—all chirped up with their replies. And still the responses came: from Garda officers and alcoholics, butchers and editors, poets and prisoners who had made good, together with farmers, dentists, cattle-jobbers, professional gamblers, and my single genius who still lives in his beloved bog.

Look, there's a lad who came down in flames over the Rhineland; beside him is a boy who parachuted down over Arnhem and lived to tell the tale. The shivering veteran of Viet Nam is there to answer "Anseo" to the posthumous calling of his name. And there too are the precious few who had found life unbearable and wrote *Finis* to their own mortal story.

A knock at the classroom door. "You're to come up now, sir." "Goodbye, Mr Chips," I murmur as I leave the room for the last time.

Just outside the classroom door are a couple of American tourists. They apologise for the intrusion; the man asks if I knew of his grandfather, a native of the town. Somewhat preoccupied, I say, "Yes, he went to San Francisco in 1908 to rebuild that city after it had been damaged in an earthquake." The tourists register surprise. I pass on.

The hall is crowded. I gesture quietly to my wife and sons. I make my way to the stage. When it comes to my turn to reply to what has been said about me I mentally warn myself not to be maudlin. The television lamps stroke over us in brilliant light. I find myself quoting Yeats. Attitudinising, I suppose.

Never to have lived is best, ancient writers say,
Never to have drawn the breath of life, never to have looked into the
eye of day.

The second best's a gay good-night
and quickly turn away.

As a lover of life this is not my philosophy at all. I say it anyway. It sounds well. Especially the "quickly turn away" part.

As I leave the building there is a crowd around the school gate. Neighbours and parents shake hands with me and wish me luck. Flanked by a pair of my grandchildren, I walk home.

The old storyteller at the winter fireside always finished his tale with a wry comment. "That's my story for you. And if there's a lie in it—let it stand."

ALSO BY BRYAN MACMAHON

in Poolbeg

The Honeyspike

---

in Children's Poolbeg

Patsy-O

Mascot Patsy-O